MONEY, MEANING
AND
BEYOND

27 Unexpected Ways to Create What *Really* Matters for Business Owners

Andrea J. Lee & Tina Forsyth

Money, Meaning and Beyond
Copyright © 2006 by Andrea J. Lee & Tina Forsyth

All rights reserved. This book, or parts thereof, may not be reproduced in any form without written permission of the author except for the inclusion of brief quotations in a review.

Published by:

MP Press, A division of
Femme Osage Publishing
1301 Colby Drive
Saint Peters, Missouri, USA 63376
www.FemmeOsagePublishing.com
Publisher@FemmeOsagePublishing.com

Printed in the United States of America

ISBN: 0-9728940-6-3

Library of Congress Control Number: 2006925496

First Printing 2006

Author Contact:
Andrea J. Lee
Suite 152, 1919B - 4 Street SW
Calgary, AB T2S 1W4
(403) 615-1237
support@msoci.com

Tina Forsyth
Suite 152, 1919B - 4 Street SW
Calgary, AB T2S 1W4
(403) 830-4339
tina@onlinebusinessmanager.com

Dedication

This book is dedicated to our clients and the privilege of serving you...

And our families and friends, who put the 'meaning' in our lives.

Acknowledgements

This book got its start from laughter. It was the laughter that burst out each time we told a story, used a metaphor, or drew an offbeat mental picture to illustrate a business concept. Each time someone around us laughed, we realized our off-the-wall way of talking about business was helping them get concepts that had previously been difficult or just plain boring.

Along this path we have to thank everyone who has laughed with us. In doing so, you have helped create a new body of business-building material that we hope helps many thousands of others – and maybe changes the way we all look at what's possible in business and in our lives.

In particular, thank you to our clients of the past several years including:

- The readers of the online newsletters 'Creating What Matters' and 'Online Business Manager: Sneak a Peek Over My Shoulder.' Thank you for your continued comments and insights, and the opportunity to serve you.

- The members of the 'Multiple Streams of Coaching Income' online community who continue to inspire us as you build your businesses.

- The members of the 'Dream Team' Virtual Assistance community who take the ideas and theory and put them into action. Thank you for your dedication.

- Clients of 'Online Business Manager,' your big vision and enlightened determination energize us.

- The 'Multiple Streams' Coaching Team of dynamite coaches who walk their talk and take their dose of 'hair of the dog' every day.

- And most recently, the business owners of all stripes who watched the 'Money and Meaning Movie'. You made it clear that you're seeking much more than money in your businesses and we look forward to exploring this path with you more.

We'd also like to single out for thanks the following truly remarkable team members:

Kerri Martin, Ericka Loften, Cindy Greenway, Joe Taylor Jr., Andy Wibbels, Carmen Guerra and KC Christensen-Lang.

Last but not least, thank you too, to the good folk we think of as 'friends of' the 'Money, Meaning & Beyond' project.

Jan MacGregor, Elyse Killoran, Suzanne Falter-Barns, Candye Hinton, Lable Braun, Anna Dargitz, Valerie Green, Tom Heck, Jillian Middleton, Kelli McCauley, Sarah & Scott Van Male and Lynne & Larry Klippel.

Important Reader's Guidelines

As you read this book, you may find that your creative juices start to open up. In anticipation of this, we recommend you choose a place to 'collect' your new thoughts – a new notebook, a document or file on your computer or perhaps a special journal.

There, we encourage you to freely list the new possibilities that start occurring to you, as well as the dots you start to connect. You might write down single words or complete streams of consciousness, and it wouldn't surprise us if you start writing upside down and in lots of different colors. In any case, however you set up your 'collection system', it will help harness the energy you're about to generate.

One other thing we hope you remember is, the creativity you're about to plug into is not going anywhere. If the rush of expanding your mind about possibilities is new to you, you might feel worried that you won't be able to recreate it. We're asking you to trust us. You will.

Just one more thing. Do not – we repeat – *please, do not* try to put all your new ideas on your 'To Do' list. We've seen too many business owners try to, and fall down from sheer exhaustion as a result.

In the end, you will add to your list of things to do, but not in a way that's hazardous to your health. Instead, like collecting drippings in a gravy pan, put your creative thoughts in a separate place where they can serve you best.

Table of Contents

Acknowledgements   5

Important Reader's Guidelines   9

Introduction   17

M O N E Y

Chapter 1 : Pink Spoons and Ice Cream   23
Ever scratch your head about how this thing called a 'business' works? If you've ever bought ice cream, you can understand what it takes to grow your biz.

Chapter 2: Desire Lines   35
Get out of the rut of (stubbornly) selling (only) what you're selling. Shift into the mindset of selling what your clients most want, by looking for their desire lines.

Chapter 3: The Multiple Streams Funnel   45
Are you making money, but only dribs and drabs and with no rhyme or reason? Organize things so clients – and money – flow to you like water through a funnel.

Chapter 4: What Is the Fastest Path to Money?   53
What one thing aren't you doing, that's blocking the flow of money to your door? Read this chapter only if you're ready to act.

Chapter 5: Get Permission to Keep in Touch   67
Long-term relationships with your most valuable clients are forged over time. Make certain your business is set up to keep in touch.

Chapter 6: A Confused Mind Always Says No   75
Are you scaring away clients by overwhelming them? Focus on one thing at a time and watch your results skyrocket.

Chapter 7: It's Not What You Say, It's How You Say It   85
How do you build a relationship with folks online, without it consuming tons of time?

Chapter 8: Nagging Your Way to Success   97
Are you a little shy of marketing, especially through repeat emails or calls? It's called 'being a loving nag' and we know you have what it takes – especially if you're a parent, or have ever been a child.

Review and Recap - Money   105
You've been reading this book because you're looking for something. Let's pause for a moment here and check to see if you've found it.

Chapter 9: **Mad Science** — 109
Do you know your numbers? Sales, expenses, the hours you work? How about how much you'd like to earn this year? If you said 'no,' you're not alone, but not for long...

Chapter 10: **The Money Game** — 117
As your plans and energy towards your business ebb and flow as they naturally will, part of the beauty of the Money Game is that you'll be able to adjust.

MEANING

Chapter 11: **Gravy Pans** — 127
Got tons to do, and not enough time? Just like how gravy gets made as a byproduct of roasting a chicken – you're getting more done than you think.

Chapter 12: **No Great Thing Is Accomplished Alone** — 137
Together we know everything and everyone, and can do everything we're meant to do through collaboration. So learn to give first, and you will receive.

Chapter 13: **Picking the Ripe Apples** — 149
Are you too smart for your own good? Stop making things complicated for yourself. It all starts with picking the ripe apples.

Chapter 14: **Excuse Me, Will You Be My Google?**   155
Want an easy business-building strategy for a change? Like Disc Jockeys of another era, your clients are looking to you to be their filter.

Chapter 15: **The Lone Ranger Syndrome**   163
Is your brain about to burst from all the little details? The right help at the right price will clear your head and rekindle the pleasure of being in business.

Chapter 16: **Salad Bowls**   175
Too tired all the time for this to be sustainable? When whisking a salad dressing, a good bowl makes all the diffeence to your wrist. Who (and what) are you leaning on?

Chapter 17: **The Clay is Never Dry**   183
Can't seem to get started? Trapped in procrastination? Focus on completion, not perfection.

Chapter 18: **Seeking the Minimum Level**   189
Would you use a power tool to put in a tack? Time and energy are your precious resources. Use them wisely by seeking the minimal level.

Review and Recap – Meaning   197
Before you move on to the 'Beyond' section of the book, let's stop for a moment to refresh what's gone before.

BEYOND

Chapter 19: **Pulling a Costanza** — 201
When you're stuck, stop. Turn yourself around and try doing the opposite.

Chapter 20: **Where Are You Coming From?** — 209
Are people ignoring you and what your business has to say? Break through the sound barrier with examples from an enlightened Golf Course.

Chapter 21: **Time for Some Hair of the Dog** — 219
Ever feel like a fraud in your biz? Or, just stuck in a rut - again? Whatever your business is, if you're embarrassed or shy about it, it's just not going to work long term. Time for some hair of the dog.

Chapter 22: — 227
How Does Your Sex Life Affect Your Business?
Want more money? Sure, mom may blush, but if you really want to earn more, you gotta play more. After all, a full and ecstatic life is the only real reason to be in business.

Chapter 23: **Riding the Tiger** — 233
Just about to make it big? But feeling stressed and unsure, maybe even scared witless about the future? Loosen up and ride the tiger.

Chapter 24: **Care to 'BOP' Your Market in the Head?** 243
If you're going to be in business, be in business all the way – be a leader in your market.

Chapter 25: **The Sun and the Wind** 251
Sick of trying so hard? Are you being the sun or the wind?

Chapter 26: **The Paul Principle** 257
Wondering if there's a true-blue 'secret' to business success? For better or worse, it's all about you.

Chapter 27: **Re-learning How to Swim** 265
Been doing things the same way for forever? Just like this story about swimming, could it be time to destroy old habits and create some new?

A Final Recap - Beyond 273
All good things must come to an end, and that includes this book! Before moving on, let's do a final recap.

Practically Speaking, What's Next? 277

In Conclusion 279

Additional Resources, Tools & Invitations 285

Endnotes 293

About the Authors 311

Introduction

Five frogs are sitting on a fence.
Two decide to jump off the fence.
How many frogs are left on the fence?

Answer: Five.[1]

Explanation: Deciding is not doing. Deciding to do something, while powerful, is still only deciding.

'Doing' is about something else.

Some people say it's about coming from the heart. We say it's about connecting the head with the heart. Or, something else entirely.

In much the same way as your leg spontaneously swings out when the doctor hits just the right spot on your knee, there's something special about when a frog - or a person - decides to do something…and then does it.

But if deciding alone doesn't do the trick, what does?
We don't pretend to have the complete answer to this. But this much we know for sure.

This book isn't an ordinary book about success. If fact, in some ways it's the antithesis. You won't find lists of steps, for example, but instead there are lots of open-ended questions for you to engage with. (Exception: the last chapter.)

The basic premise is that there are three important parts to making business (and life) work.

First, there are the Basic Facts. Information. You know, the stuff that forms the bulk of many business textbooks. What is profit? What constitutes expenses? How does ROI, or return on investment, work?

Second, there is the 'Who Cares?' part. Why do these business facts matter to you? When you're in the trenches networking your heart out for new customers, or trying to set up a computer system, how does any theoretical business concept impact you, today?

And third, there is the 'Greater Truth' part. Making a livelihood is of course one of the most common reasons for someone to become a business owner. But our contention is that underneath that simple 'why' is something deeper that goes beyond the default: "Honey, I'm working through supper again because we have to pay the bills."

We invite you to think about it for a moment.

In our experience, the deeper reason or greater truth about dreaming of something more, of going beyond what you might think possible for your business and your life, is much more accessible in ways *not* laid out in most books about business.

When working with our clients, we often call these access points 'side doors.' These are the sneaky indirect doorways that often make it easier and more enjoyable for adult, human business owners to understand something, begin to relate to it in a personal way, and then – almost involuntarily – begin to live it without effort.

It's about seeing things differently. And relating to your business differently. It's definitely about plugging into more money. And, it's about thinking, doing and being. Not just deciding.

Like the little rubber hammer the doctor uses to access the muscle in your knee, there are tools, insights and stories to help you respond naturally in ways that support your business. We call these things wisdom, and you don't have to have an MBA to get some.

So, think of the stuff in the chapters that follow as a series of wise little hammers for your business reflexes.

Pick up reading at the beginning, middle or end – wherever you feel called - and along the way, begin transforming your relationship with your business and your life.

MONEY

"The world is awash in money! Do you hear what that means? It is awash in money. It is flowing for everyone. It is like Niagara Falls. And most of you are showing up with your teaspoons."

Abraham-Hicks

CHAPTER 1
Pink Spoons and Ice Cream

Ever scratch your head about how this thing called a 'business' works? If you've ever bought ice cream, you can understand what it takes to grow your biz.

1

As you'll discover throughout this book, we are big believers in the power of metaphor to understand complex things.

You know the saying, "You can't solve a problem with the same mind that created it?"[1] Metaphors are ways to get out of our 'old' mind and look at things differently.

In terms of building a business, we've found it very useful to describe how a business works in terms of Ice Cream.

Whether this is your first business or your fifth; regardless of if you own a moving company or do taxes for a living, there is something in this metaphor that can help.

Let's begin.

> *Imagine for a moment it's a hot sunny day, and you are in an ice cream store. And what a great one it is. There are so many flavors – it looks like over 100! You don't seem to remember there being this much choice when you were a kid! And look...all the smiling faces behind the counter are waiting for you. Time to make a decision.*

Well, this flavor looks like it could be good. Are those pecans or walnuts in there? On second thought, this one over here is neat looking with all the fruity colors. Hmm.

What's that? Would I like to try a flavor – no charge? Sure I would…how many can I try? Okay well, let's try this one, and that one and just one more…over here. Hey these little Pink Spoon samples are a great idea! Okay, I know what I'd like. I'll have a scoop of this kind now and I'll take a small carton of this other one home.

At this point, if you decide to stop reading for a moment and go get yourself some ice cream, we don't blame you…go right ahead! But promise us just one thing before you set this book down. Make sure that when you go into the ice cream store, you observe what's going on underneath the surface using your new X-ray goggles.

You see, no matter what flavor you chose in the imaginative exercise we just did, it's important to us that you take a moment to anchor the metaphor in your mind. If you do, we think you'll find even more valuable lessons about money and your business than what we write about in black and white. These are the lessons 'in between the lines.'

So going back to the experience of choosing a flavor of ice cream in your imagination. Tastes pretty darned good, right?
What if you could create an experience much like the one you've just imagined, for people who walk into your 'store?'

What if their experience of spending money with you could be as painless and pleasurable?

It doesn't matter if you have a physical store, you run your business from an office building, or perhaps your 'store' is a completely virtual one, with people who visit you strictly on the Internet. Experience tells us if you're willing to look beneath the surface of the metaphor, there are a dozen connections you can make that can bring your business more money.

The central one we want to start out with is the idea of a Pink Spoon.

First, what is a Pink Spoon, exactly and why should you care?

(Li la little)

In the case of the ice cream store, a Pink Spoon is the tiny little utensil you get when you ask to taste a flavor before you buy. They're not always Pink Spoons – they can be tiny wooden paddles sometimes – but one of our favorite ice cream stores uses Pink Spoons, so we like to use that name for them.

What's more important than the name is the concept behind it. It's simple, really. Give away a small taste of something you are selling, for free, and if done right, more often than not, earn a paying client as a result.

Great Pink Spoons have 5 main characteristics.

1. They are free.
2. They are compelling and sought after.
3. They are small in size, a true sample.
4. They are easy for the business owner to give away, don't require an ongoing time commitment to deliver, and aren't too costly to be wise.
5. They are a natural lead in to the core product or service you want to sell.

CASE STUDY:

ANDREA

My local florist sent me a card offering a single rose – for free – on Mother's Day. In simple and direct language, the card said, "Pick Up One Free Long-Stemmed Rose on Mother's Day – You choose the color."

While picking up my free rose, I asked the store owner how the Pink Spoon offer was going. (She didn't think of it as a Pink Spoon then, but it was.)

She said it was one of her biggest earners of the year – when husband's would come in and buy a dozen roses for their wife and – by the way – claim the thirteenth one for free.

Nosy as I am, I congratulated her and asked if that meant she was crazy just one day of the year, or did it help her long term business, to which she replied:

"Oh no. Husbands are real creatures of habit. They come back for birthdays, or for other occasions because they know us now. And we make it really easy to come back…"

CASE STUDY:

We often get asked for ideas for great Pink Spoons for service businesses. The answer is usually: Either a party or something that educates your market.

A simple brochure, pamphlet, online ecourse or other format containing the top 5 reasons why your service is essential, can often do the trick.

'5 Things to Know About Whitening Your Teeth'

'5 Most Common Reasons Plumbing Emergencies Happen.'

Or, a great case study is one of our favorite magazines called, 'Worthwhile: Work with Passion, Purpose and Profit'.[2] How have they given away a taste of their intangible offering – a magazine?

Answer: A content-rich website in the form of a blog[3] and podcasts[4] which cover topics such as 'Building a Green Career,' 'Good Profits versus Bad' and 'God at Work.' Last we heard, it was working well…they're now circulating over 100,000 copies per issue. Why not check it out for yourself? It's 'worth' it.

Wisdom Nugget:

Are you starting to ask yourself how you can apply the Pink Spoon model to your own business? Or maybe you're already offering the equivalent of a Pink Spoon. Great! Write your thoughts down here so you can come back to them later.

Now let's pin down just a few more observations about this thing called a Pink Spoon.

1. Notice that in this model, the more people who try a Pink Spoon – whether that be a rose, taste of ice cream, or something else – it makes sense that the people will likely go ahead and purchase something.

    In the ice cream world, a Pink Spoon can lead to a single scoop of ice cream. Which in turn can lead to a pint or litre of ice cream. And sometimes that can even lead to a regular customer who buys an ice cream cake every couple of months for their children.

    And so on.

It all starts with a free taste, though, right? The more Pink Spoons are given out, the more sales and the better for the business.

2. Notice too that as the ice cream customer moves from free Pink Spoon, to ice cream, to pint, to an even more expensive ice cream cake, etc., many things are happening.

   They are spending more money for one thing. And that's a great thing…

   Can you also see that they're building a <u>relationship with the company? A sense of comfort and familiarity is created that goes beyond a simple transaction.</u>

3. As well, let's not forget that some people may never buy anything more than an ice cream cone, and you may run into some that take a few Pink Spoons and leave! That's more than okay.

4. Last but not least for now, consider the fact that sometimes after ordering the same single scoop for years, the customer might go back to the beginning and try a few more Pink Spoons.

   This is very cool! In fact, it's a great way to encourage already-loyal clients to buy more items from you more frequently.

All of these insights are part of a giant metaphor we like to refer to as the Ice Cream Journey of Business, and it looks like this:

The Pink Spoon is above the widest part of the Funnel and is by far the most critical layer. The Ice Cream Cone is next. The pint-sized containers are next again, and the bottom of the funnel is filled out with an Ice Cream Cake and the Ice Cream Flavor of the Month Club.

By this point, you can probably start to sense the truth of the statement:

If you've ever bought an ice cream, you can understand what it takes to grow your business.

Now it's your turn.

Remember: The Pink Spoon model is based on real-world success, NOT theory.

Wisdom nuggets:

Does the idea of having one or more Pink Spoons make sense to you after reading this chapter? How? Answer in the space below as it applies to your business today.

What could your first (or next) Pink Spoon be?

To brainstorm with other business owners about Pink Spoons in real-time, there is an open community online that can help.

Details are at www.MoneyMeaningandBeyond.com

For now, jot down your raw thoughts here:

CHAPTER 2
Desire Lines

Get out of the rut of (stubbornly) selling (only) what you're selling. Shift into the mindset of selling what your clients most want, by looking for their desire lines.

2

One of the most gratifying things about being in business is being able to satisfy other people's desires. If this sounds a little sexy to you, that's because it is! But not in the way you might think.

A 'desire line' is an urban planning term that refers to pathways that spring up in parks and fields when people walk where they want to walk. Desire lines like these are said to show 'yearning' on the part of the walkers, and similar desire lines occur in businesses too – your business, in fact.

Here's an example. Have you ever heard it said, "The great thing about Delicatessens is if three people ask for a sandwich that's not on the menu, they put in on the menu." We'd like for you as a business owner to start thinking a little like a Deli.

What do your customers want that you aren't currently selling? How many times have you been asked for something by a client, only to have you say 'no' and moved on to the task of trying to drum up more business?

If you're a cookie store, we suggest you immediately stock some milk. Make sense?

If you're in the self-storage business, make sure you also sell boxes. (Also cleaning services and garage sale kits.)

If you're any kind of a consultant, make extra sure you save email requests asking for just 'a few minutes of your advice about something important.'

These are naturally occurring desire lines in your business; noticing and acting on them means more money, more easily.

Jay Abraham claims there are only three ways in the world to grow a business[1]:

1. Increase the total number of customers you have.
2. Increase the price of what you sell.
3. Or increase the amount of money each customer spends with you.

Of these, the last one is most often the quickest way to increase your income and you can start by asking a single question: What would your current customers buy from you – today – if you only sold it?

Making more money really isn't hard if you're able to think of yourself as in the business of satisfying desires.

CASE STUDY:

When the profession of life coaching first came on the scene in the late 1980s, tens of thousands of people decided to become coaches for a living.

Many of these coaches struggled to find clients who wanted 'better lives' – they weren't able to make a connection with the market. Nearly 20 years later, thousands of talented coaches are earning six and seven figure incomes in businesses they love. How did this come about?

They began the exercise of watching for – and acting on - natural Desire Lines. For example:

Sales Coach Wendy Weiss, The Queen of Cold Calling[2] taps into a rich vein of desire with her multimedia home-study products for business owners such as 'Getting Past the Palace Guard' and 'Cold-Calling College.'

Personal Coach Jennifer Louden[3], connects with the deep desire modern women have to rediscover comfort through her best-selling books, among them 'The Pregnant Woman's Comfort Book,' and 'Comfort Secrets for Busy Women.'

Wisdom nuggets:

Take a moment to integrate the idea that struggle is not a requirement of a business owner. Even the most successful business owners, when they're trying to grow, can run into the idea that they 'must work hard to make more money.' So don't take for granted that you 'get it' before you pause for one more moment.

What requests have you had for additional products or services from your current customers? Which ones are you most interested in providing – directly or indirectly?

- Zeit
- Gut fühlen

Chapter 2: Desire Lines   41

→ EotK in Mini-WS!

How could you satisfy your customer's desires simply by repackaging an existing offering? There is a reason why there are dozens of types of cheese in the dairy section of the supermarket. What can you learn about repackaging from the cheese department in the grocery store?

→ Das Ding mit der Zeit.
→ laser-Coaching an
　　　- time
　　　- struggle
　　　- stress
　　　- well-being

→ Mini-Workshops für 10 €
　→ mit 10 €-Coupon für Kurz-US
→ Kurz-WS ↗ Coaching
　　　　　↘ WE-WS → Naturn-Kein

• Fragen: Was brauchst du?
　　　　 Was würde dir helfen?

Information is something that's desired in almost every corner of the business world. Use yourself as an example. Would you like more information about how to save money on taxes? Would you buy a CD-Set, eBook or home-study program from your trusted accountant on this topic? What information do you have between your ears — or that you could access in other people — to create an information product that supplements your current business?

Not sure what else your clients may want to buy from you? There is a simple way to find out – just ask! Send a short survey to your existing client base to find out their current challenges/problems… and then look for products to solve this for them.

Keep your survey questions short - in fact, we recommend asking just one quick question to get the highest response rate (the more questions you ask the less likely people are to respond). For example:

What is your biggest question about building your business online?

Or;

What is your biggest challenge in finding new clients for your business?

Use this space below to create a short survey.

CHAPTER 3
The Multiple Streams Funnel

Are you making money, but only dribs and drabs and with no rhyme or reason? Organize things so clients – and money – flow to you like water through a funnel.

3

Now that you understand the Ice Cream Journey of business, as well as the concept of Desires Lines, it's time to extrapolate this into the real, live business model.

The online business model we use is called The Multiple Streams Funnel and a version of this is behind every profitable business we've worked with. Here is what it looks like.

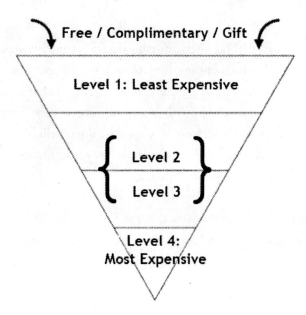

Take a moment now to draw the Funnel for yourself, on a full sheet of blank paper. This will help you start to internalize the blueprint.

Now much like the Ice Cream Journey, the Multiple Streams Funnel represents the path or "journey" your clients follow from the first time they see your brochure, visit you at your booth, or maybe look at your website.

From there, they have a choice as to whether or not to continue a relationship with you. Each time they take a purchasing step down the levels of the funnel, they are engaging further with your business.

The price points in each level are different in every market, and typically increase from level to level as you go down the funnel.

Why is this? People make buying decisions mainly based on emotion, which means that they want to feel a sense of trust/relationship with the person or company they are buying from. By starting with free gifts and moving through the funnel in price increments, your customers will be more likely to purchase at the next level as they get to know, trust and like you (and your products!).

Are you starting to see how this fits in with the Ice Cream Journey as well? Now let's go through each of the levels in a bit more detail, starting at the top:

Free/Complimentary/Gift

The Free/Complimentary/Gift level is your first (and quite often your only!) opportunity to engage with potential customers. What you want to do as this first step is offer something of value for free to people that visit your website, and give it in exchange for their contact information (name, email address and possibly mailing address).

This is THE most important and often the most overlooked step in the online marketing process, and the reason we call this model Pink Spoon Marketing™.

Because without the free/complimentary/gift level done well…you have no Pink Spoon, and you have no opportunity to gain a customer. No ice cream cone sale for you!

Level 1: The Least Expensive

At this stage your customers have received value from you in the form of a free gift, and if they liked what they received they will be open to consider a purchase at the next price level.

Levels 2 and 3: The Middle

This is where the rubber starts to meet the road so to speak, meaning that the people who purchase from you at this level have truly engaged in what you have to offer.

They have moved past the 'taste testing' level and are now willing to spend their 'thinking money' with you. (Thinking money means that they will stop to think about the purchase before buying; it's a conscious decision.)

Level 4: The Most Expensive

This level is what we like to call the 'sweet spot'. Customers who purchase at this level have a pretty good chance of becoming 'raving fans' and long term clients. The relationship is pretty strong at this point, and unless something happens to deteriorate the relationship, chances are it could open the door to such things as referrals, alliances and the like.

All because you've taken the time to cultivate a strong relationship.

Wisdom nugget:

Take a moment now to fill in your own Multiple Streams Funnel. What does it look like right now? And how would you like it to look?

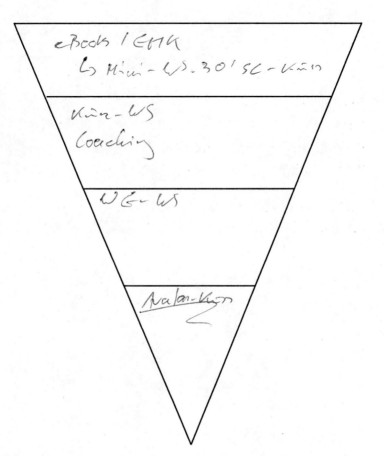

CHAPTER 4
What Is the Fastest Path to Money?

What one thing aren't you doing, that's blocking the flow of money to your door? Read this chapter only if you're ready to act.

4

It's no secret that bright people – the majority of business owners – like to create mischief for themselves, precisely because they are bright. Complicating things makes life interesting, after all! But it's not the best strategy to creating more money and meaning.

Maybe that's why the core message of this chapter is so often met with (a) a lot of resistance, (b) a case of disbelief or (c) both.

If we had our way, all business owners would ask this question of themselves and their team, at least once a month:

What is the fastest path to making money today?

Then – again if we could have our way – the business owner would make a list of the answers, choose one that resonates most and get to work.

Would you like to give it a try? Let's do a few case studies first.

CASE STUDY:

A professional trainer told us he was in a 'very bad' financial situation in his business. When we asked him, "What's very bad?" his answer was, "I have to earn $5000 in the next 2 months or I will go out of business."

Our response was the question above: What is the fastest path to making money today?

His answer: "Great. I'll think hard about that."

Being who we are, there was some silence after his reply. He then said, "Maybe I'll create a new program and see if it sells."

We repeated the question.

"What is the fastest path to making money – TODAY?"

And elaborated: "If we gave you 15 minutes to write one email to send to your existing customers, what could you sell them TODAY that would mean money in your bank account TODAY?"

Again silence. Then, "That's a good question, I'll think about it and figure it out."

And because this person wasn't in a long-term relationship with us, we are not sure what he ended up doing, if anything.

Author of 'The Art of the Start' Guy Kawasaki has this to say about making money today. In more formal business terms, this is also called 'cash flow.'

> "Focus on cash flow, not profitability. The theory is that profits are the key to survival. If you could pay the bills with theories, this would be fine. The reality is that you pay bills with cash, so focus on cash flow. If you know you are going to bootstrap, you should start a business with a small up-front capital requirement, short sales cycles, short payment terms, and recurring revenue. It means passing up the big sale that takes twelve months to close, deliver, and collect. Cash is not only king, it's queen and prince too for a bootstrapper."[1]

If you are in business for yourself and don't have a sizeable amount of money in savings as a cushion, or a husband or wife's salary you're relying on, you are a bootstrapper. A sizeable amount is the amount you need to earn in one month to live, multiplied by at least six to twelve.

Wisdom nugget:

Many – MANY – business owners complain about not earning enough money. And it's true. This has to be the number one stress point for any business owner, especially if you're new.

But here's the wisdom in this nugget. If you have been complaining about it for more than one month – not earning enough money is not really an emergency for you.

Somehow, some way, you are surviving without more money. Yet you are still complaining, or worrying, or not sleeping at night because of it.

Our advice is to either stop worrying about it because you're clearly making it somehow, or – come to realize it is truly serious and do something about it.

In coaching terms, it's common practice to say, "People do what they do, because they have nothing more compelling to do."[2] Or, as Dr. Phil would say, "Worrying about making money in your business is serving you somehow."

Only you can really know if this is true. Is it? You don't have to write your answer down, but here is some space anyway, so you can look at it while you think, if that helps.

When you're ready to do something, let's get to the question at hand.

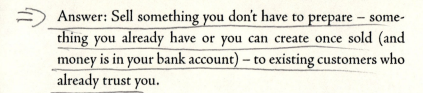 What's the fastest path to money in your business, right now?

Answer: Sell something you don't have to prepare – something you already have or you can create once sold (and money is in your bank account) – to existing customers who already trust you.

 The last part is as important as the first because you must be able to communicate with these customers today. So either you have their email address or their phone number, and you can contact them with a reasonable expectation that they will be happy you did.

If you are new in business, substitute the phrase 'to existing customers who already trust you' with 'to people you have a previous relationship who trust you.' This means people you know from your last job, social circle or professional network.

If you are a severe introvert and you claim to not know people, you really shouldn't be in business. But, we digress. Let's do another case study, shall we?

CASE STUDY:

My friend Tom Heck is a genius. He is an inventor, the best trainer I know on earth, and owner of an online business called 'Teach Me Teamwork' in which he teaches people teamwork and leadership skills in a fun and memorable way.[3]

Tom's been building this business for several years and gets testimonials just about daily from customers telling him about results you and I dream about. At the time of this writing, Tom has 23,505 Members in 97 Countries. (If your business has anything to do with developing a list of online subscribers, it's worth checking out his website.)

The thing is though; I recently had a conversation with Tom about money. You guessed it – I asked him the fateful question about money, and earning it, and how could he do it today.

Where Tom's example is different though is that he actually acted. He hung up the phone from talking with me and sat with his wife Anne to create an email inviting his existing customers to take advantage of a special offer.

In fact, this was the subject line of his email: 'Save on Teambuilding Resources - Act Now!'

When I saw this email, I was completely, completely elated. I wrote to him right away:

> way to go tom! :)

His reply?

> Our conversation last night inspired me. I walked upstairs and talked with Anne. We put this CD offer together last night.

On Mar 29, 2006, at 3:51 PM, [Andrea Lee] wrote:

> cool! :)
>
> so how well did this email do? :)

-----Original Message-----
From: Tom Heck
Sent: Wednesday, March 29, 2006 9:27 PM

> This email has generated about $2,500 in sales in about 24 hours. One person who is Australian bought 7 sets (about $700 sale)!
>
> We are sending out a reminder email tomorrow to let people know the special 5 CD sale is over on Friday night at midnight. I'd like to see an additional $2,500 in sales.

And then again, two days later:

-----Original Message-----
From: Tom Heck
Sent: Friday, March 31, 2006 12:55 PM

Hi Andrea --

Wow! Where has this day gone?!

We sent out a 'last chance' email yesterday (you probably saw it) and we've been receiving orders all day. We've passed $7,000 in sales from this one promotional!

This is incredible. The offer expires tonight and we still have sales to come from Asia.

We've said it before and we'll say it again – Tom's experience proves what we know for sure. <u>There is money waiting to be made in every business that offers a quality service.</u> Especially if you've been 'surviving' in business for at least a little while, we're confident enough to say without even meeting you that you can do the equivalent of what Tom did – on a smaller or larger scale.

You just have to be willing to answer the one question:

What's the fastest path to money for you today? Make a list. Act on the one that feels right.

'Act on' means nothing more or less than 'ask for the business.' You must build the fortitude, courage, and/or habit to ask for the business. Lucky thing, you can read the chapter on 'loving nagging' later in the book for a shift in that arena.

Wisdom nugget:

If you don't have a way of being in touch with your customers via email, RSS, telephone or even the slightly slower regular mail, the next chapter is for you.

Read on for a new way of looking at the relevance of relationships in your business – 100% critical if you want money and meaning, sustainably in your business.

In the meantime, use the space on the next page to express the thoughts in your head – whatever shape they're in right now – about this chapter.

Chapter 4: What is the Fastest Path to Money?

What's your fastest path to money, today? Will you behave like the gentleman in the first Case Study, or like Tom, in the second? This is your space.

CHAPTER 5
Get Permission to Keep in Touch

Long-term relationships with your most valuable clients are forged over time. Make certain your business is set up to keep in touch.

5

In a book of mindset shifts and side doors, this chapter should stand out for its simple straightforwardness.

If you aren't yet asking for permission[1] to keep in touch with clients and future clients, start now.

Remember, you do need to get permission to communicate with people, especially in the online world... otherwise you will be perceived as sending SPAM email, which of course you don't want to do!

Specifically, you can collect[2]:

- names and email addresses, or
- names and physical mailing addresses, or
- both.

Be sure to get permission, and then once you have it, use it by being in touch at least 2-3 times each month, with something of value to say.

Wisdom Nugget:

Here are some examples of things that could be of value.

- A web design business could send out a weekly online newsletter sharing tips on how to get the best web design for the best price.

- A daycare center could create a mini online course on the most important things to do, to prepare your child for daycare.

- A financial advisor could generate a weekly bulletin with the week's stock tips.

Each of these is an example of an effective Pink Spoon, which we covered in more detail in Chapter 1.

The goal is to create a Pink Spoon that isn't just valuable - but irresistible - to the people who are most likely to become your paying clients down the road. That is the winning formula you're after.

People will happily give you their contact information in order to receive something they care about. As a result, growing the number of people on your list becomes a relatively easy process.

CASE STUDY:

My husband Mike and I have plans to purchase land overseas. Somewhere we can grow fresh fruit in our backyard, go snorkeling out the front door, continue to pursue our business pursuits and watch our investment grow.

To this end, I found an organization called International Living[3], a web-based business dedicated to helping people find the best opportunities to invest in a new home or a new life, start a new business or invest in the future, overseas.

The website was very professional, but I wasn't sure if it was trustworthy. Our plans are significant and important to us, so I decided to sign up for their 'International Living Daily e-Letter' to get to know them.

After 6 months of truly helpful e-Letters, I paid for a one-hour class on how to start a business overseas. It was a terrific class and I have a great deal of respect for the entertaining, thorough and genuine care they take in their business.

The time is coming when Mike and I will want to shortlist the countries we want to investigate. I'm quite sure we'll go on a tour with International Living, and have them introduce us to local real estate

> agents and attorneys. Short of having family or friends to help us instead, I've come to know, like and trust this company and really look forward to what's possible with their help.

If you're in the business of providing a service such as the above, especially one that is a significant long-term investment, consider the above case study very seriously. There's simply no better way we know of to cultivate this kind of client than by wooing them through information. Just make sure it's immediately valuable to them, and they've given you permission to send it.

By the way, the most recent statistics on the International Living Daily e-Letter? More than 270,000 eager readers receive it daily. You can bet they never miss a chance to build that list of readers, because it pays.

Remember: people do business with people they know, like and trust. Start putting in place a system by which you can stay in touch.

CASE STUDY:

> Here's a conversation we had recently:
>
> Tina: I found this really cool site about swimming. You should see it.

Andrea: Yeah? What's the site?

Tina: TotalImmersion.net[4]. The videos are really neat. I think I'll try the drills and see if I can improve my time for my next triathlon. Supposedly they teach you to swim as much like a fish as humanly possible.

Andrea: Cool.

Tina: Doh! They don't have anything I can sign up for at their website! I hate that!

Andrea: Ugh! I hate that too. You should write and tell them.

Tina: Too bad.

Andrea: Yep, too bad.

In chapter 27 of this book, you'll hear more about Total Immersion Swimming and how Tina's experience with it brought another important lesson to light.

For now, let us leave you with this thought:

If you're not assertively getting permission to stay in touch with people who are naturally interested in you, you are turning business away.

There are people who are eager to do business with you – in significant dollar amounts - that you aren't connecting with yet.

How long will you keep them waiting?

Use this space to list 3 ways you can pursue more money in your business in the next 90 days.

If you have more than 3 ideas, go ahead and list them all. Then go back and circle the 3 you'd like to do first. We're looking for ways in which you can add real money in the next 30, 60 and 90 days. Go for it!

CHAPTER 6
A Confused Mind Always Says No

Are you scaring away clients by overwhelming them?
Focus on one thing at a time and
watch your results skyrocket.

6

This may be a hard question to answer. But if you're as determined as we think you are to build a business that's profitable and meaningful, you'll take a good hard look in the mirror now and answer:

Are you scaring away clients by overwhelming them?

If you answered 'yes' or 'maybe,' this chapter is for you.

Confusing clients is an astoundingly common business mistake – fixing it can lead to 'found' income in the order of tens of thousands of dollars each year.

You see, a confused mind always says no. If you think you might be confusing clients, you are helping them say 'no' to doing business with you.

So what can you do to make it easy to do business with you instead?

When communicating with your clients, cultivate the habit of having only one 'call to action' and you will see a marked increase in your results. This applies to all your advertising, promotions as well as your website.

In fact, far too many businesses spend money on a far-too-fancy website that confuses the visitor, resulting in nothing. No business, no potential for business – only overwhelm and frustration. Oh yes, don't forget the unnecessarily large bill for the over-designed website.

Wisdom Nugget:

When you walk up to a mailbox, it's very clear what to do because there is only one thing available TO do. The mailbox's existence is the epitome of focus.

So what do you, as a 'customer' of the mailbox do? You pull on the handle and put the mail in.

When it's clear to a customer what they're supposed to do, it's much more likely they will do it.

If you're thinking this message is about keeping it simple, you're right on the money.

This is how clear and direct we want it to be for your clients to do business with you:

- "Oh, there's a special on this week. I'll call this toll-free number now."

- "My massage therapist does hot stone therapy now? I better book 3 sessions for the price of 2 before that expires."

- "There are 3 coaching slots open, I better buy one of those right away."

Let's go into some more depth when it comes to websites whose job it is to make you money.[1]

What 'one action step' do you want visitors to take when they visit your website?

If you've read the previous chapter on 'Getting Permission' you know that often the answer is: provide their email address in exchange for a valuable piece of information in the form of a Pink Spoon.

If they give you their email, it doesn't matter how much longer they spend on your website because you have the ability to keep in touch.

Depending on your business, there may be a different 'action step' that you want people to take. Just be sure that you are capturing their contact information in some way.

Then once you've decided on the ONE main action step that you want people to take, you can design your website using the philosophy of the 'one-Banana.'[2]

A 'one-Banana' website is a website where you offer the visitor just one next step to take. (One banana instead of a bunch!)

Instead of having a myriad of menu links and different pages that people get lost in, make your site is super simple - allowing the visitor to understand the one thing they should do.

CASE STUDY:

> Take a look at this part of a web page[3] created by Stephi Stewart, Author of 'Fire Your Wedding Planner'
>
> **Learn My Wedding Saving Secrets...**
>
> Just use your *first name*, *valid email* and *wedding date* - then click "Free Instant Access!" to enter the site and begin your FREE Wedding Planning Course by eMail...
>
> First Name: [   ]
> eMail: [   ]
> Wedding Date: [September 2005 ▼]
>
> [Free Instant Access!]
>
> The site has a purpose that is clear as day – gather email addresses in exchange for valuable information. As such, the site is designed equally simply.

In fact, the site is compelling in its simplicity. If a visitor is getting married in the near future, there is nothing – no distractions, confusion or overwhelm – to stop them from filling in their name and email address and clicking the 'one banana'.

Stephi's button labeled 'Free Instant Access' is a clear one- banana - a beacon to the visitor looking for what to do - and it works.

Wisdom Nugget:

As you travel the Internet, keep your eyes peeled for the kind of clarity we're talking about in this chapter. Which sites confuse and overwhelm you – as a visitor – and result in you doing nothing? What sites are so simple and clear that you know exactly what to do?

What can you learn from your responses to each and how will you let your own wisdom guide the design of your website?

Note that the one-Banana style of web page design is counter-intuitive to many web designers. And by embracing this approach you'll dramatically change the relationship you have with yours. This is for a couple of reasons.

- First, most web designers are not marketers, they're artists.

Their idea of a good website is one that, 'looks pretty.'

And while there's nothing wrong with artists or looking pretty, we think you'll agree when we say we don't care if your site is ugly as long as it brings you business. (If it looks lovely, that's a great by product.)

+ Second, the simplicity of the one-banana approach often means you no longer need the skills of a sophisticated web designer. Anyone with basic HTML skills such as a Virtual Assistant[4] can create a one-banana site.

By focusing on just one thing on your website, you may find you not only increase sales, but decrease your web design expenses too.

Remember: A confused mind always says no.

Each time you go to communicate with your customers, ask whether you are overwhelming them or not.

Keep your website clean and focused, so the only thing a person can do at your site is give you their email address.

Then, once you have their email address you can keep in touch and start to build a relationship that turns visitors into clients.

Chapter 6: A Confused Mind Always Says No

Wisdom Nugget:

As a business owner, this is one of the most important habits we'd like you to get into. Collect examples of great websites, advertisements and any other kind of promotion. Keep a file – whether that's in your desk drawer, in a folder in your email program, or somewhere else entirely – use this as a starting off point when you go to connect with your clients.

If you already have something like this, make a pact with yourself to use it at least once or twice a month.

Part of creating what matters to you in life is working smart. Don't reinvent the wheel. Keep a 'Samples File' so you can piggyback on successful promotions done by others. Add your own flair, and away you go.

What are you going to promote this month?

What clear offer could you make to your clients this week?

How could you streamline your websites and emails to follow the one-banana philosophy?

CHAPTER 7
It's Not What You Say, It's How You Say It

How do you build a relationship with folks online, without it consuming tons of time?

7

Dear Tina,

How do you build a relationship with folks online, without it consuming tons of time?

Terri Z, Founder, Solo-e.com"[1]

This is a great question...for the simple fact that it means Terri 'gets' the importance of building a relationship.

Online or off, relationships build businesses. And if you aren't already taking advantage of building more of the right ones using the Internet, you should – it's just too efficient and effective to overlook.

So let's talk a little more about Terri's question.

We've said it before and we'll say it again, if you aren't willing to put in the time and energy required to build a relationship with your visitors or subscribers online, we dare say don't even bother. We take a rather hard stance on this.

What are some of the best ways to do this without consuming tons of your time?

Do note that it will require *some* of your time. However a little goes a long way — if you use of the right tools and technology. How cool is that?

There are 2 important elements to building a relationship, online or offline.

First, you mush **REACH OUT** to a person.

And second, they must **RESPOND** to you.

Until both of these steps have taken place - reach and respond - the relationship hasn't actually started yet.

It's like being hit on by someone when you're at the bar. If some guy comes up and says, "Hey baby, what's your sign?" and you walk away without responding, the 'relationship' has ended before it ever began.

(It's been a while since we've been in the bar scene, have the lines gotten any better since then?)

Using the above as an example, it becomes easy to see that as we build relationships in our business, the objective should be to **REACH** out to people in such a way that is mostly likely to get a **RESPONSE**.

Chapter 7: It's Not What You Say, It's How You Say It

You want to start with the end in mind, so first decide what kind of response you want to get. Desired responses could be:

- getting someone to read your newsletter
- getting someone to participate in your survey
- getting someone to make a purchase from you
- getting someone to send you a referral
- etc...

If you first get clear on what kind of response you want, it's easier to decide on the best way to reach out.

This is where the power of the Internet comes into play, giving you the ability to reach out using online tools that are automated and allow you to reach many people with 'just a click'.

Let's take a look at a three examples of how we can REACH out to people:

1. Autoresponders

An Autoresponder is a fancy name for a software program that can send email messages on your behalf, when you tell it to.

A great way to reach out to a lot of people without spending a lot of time is to set-up a series of email messages that your Autoresponder sends out each time someone makes a purchase.

If you work primarily in the offline world, this would be the equivalent of sending a card that says 'thank you for your business' each time they visited you.

One of our favorite Autoresponder strategies is what we like to call the 'Quick Question' email. This is a short email that could look something like this:

> Hi Tanya,
>
> Thanks so much for joining 'peek over my shoulder', it's great to have you on board.
>
> I was wondering, what is your biggest question about building your business online?
>
> Let me know...
>
> Thanks!
>
> Tina Forsyth
> www.OnlineBusinessManager.com
> tina@onlinebusinessmanager.com

This is exactly what people receive when they first sign up for the Online Business Manager newsletter. It's the first REACH out to them, and does a great job of making a connection as well as gathering valuable feedback.

In our experience over half of the people who get this simple question take the time to respond, giving us the opportunity to reply to them and start a deeper relationship.

2. Newsletter or Ezine

Another great way to reach out to people is by sending a newsletter - also known as an ezine, in online terms - on a regular basis. Again, keep in mind here that your objective is to get a RESPONSE from your readers, so before you sit down to write each issue, ask yourself, "What kind of response do I want to get today?"

This could be as simple as writing an article and asking for their input on a certain topic, or offering a product for sale. Yes, inviting them to buy something from you qualifies as reaching out for a response!

When it comes to building a relationship through the Internet, keep in mind that your subject line can make a big difference. Instead of saying 'Newsletter Issue IV' for example, give some thought to how you can entice people to read what you have to say, and respond as well, based on your subject line alone.

CASE STUDY:

ANDREA

My newsletter called 'Creating What Matters' is a great example of one of the ways I build relationships with thousands of people at a time.

The goal has almost become a bit of a game; I love reaching out and seeing how many people respond to each issue, because the more people 'talking back' means I'm on the right track to providing value.

Here are some examples of the subject lines I've had the greatest response to:

- 'Nip and Tuck' for Your Ezine
- Does Orange + Pink = The New Green?
- How to Un-crap Your Day
- Hearts, Heads & Stars: 'Save the Date'
- Eye, Ear & Brain Candy

3. No-Fee Teleseminars

One final way to build a relationship with lots of people at once is through Teleseminars. A Teleseminar is a seminar by telephone. You and between 10-500 other people from all over the world call a regular phone number and discuss the topic of the day. If you decide to use a Teleseminar as a reach out technique, you are the host of the call and will lead it.[2]

Offering a complimentary Teleseminar to your clients and potential clients is one of the best ways we know to strengthen an online relationship. There's just something about a live voice that people love – a Teleseminar can instantly strengthen the relationship depth and intimacy.

If your goal is to build quality relationships online, it is very doable with just the above three techniques. Which one will you try out first?

Wisdom Nugget:

What other methods of reaching out can you think of? Could you hold an Open House Day at your business, or perhaps a wine and cheese reception? How about thank you cards, birthday cards or a gift on another special occasion? Online or off, the strategy is the same…in a world where people crave connection – it's not what you say to, it's how you say it – regularly, personally and with sincerity – that counts.

Lest we forget, before moving on, we want to make sure to address the **RESPONSE** part of relationship building. Remember, we stated earlier that unless you **REACH** out and get a **RESPONSE**, there is no relationship.

We strongly recommend responding to all of your emails, even if just to say 'thanks for your input'. Remember, it is at the point of response that the relationship starts, so this is **KEY!**

People really do appreciate knowing their email has been read, and it can make a **HUGE** difference in the depth of relationship that you create.

Yes, we can hear you groan as you read this, "But I already get enough email. How am I possibly supposed to respond to every email that comes in?"

Here are just a couple of tips to keep your sanity in check:

- Keep your replies really short. Use 2-3 sentences as a general rule of thumb.

- Write as you speak. Don't get hung up in grammar; just be you. Remember that communication is the transfer of emotion and it's not so much what you say in perfect sentences as how you convey the emotion.

- Create a few stock replies that you use frequently so you can simply personalize them before sending.

- Consider hiring a Virtual Assistant to help. With a bit of training that person can help answer on your behalf and become part of your commitment to developing relationships.

We hope this answers Terri Z's most excellent question. In summary, let's recap this simple formula:

Reach + Response = Relationship

If you can build this formula into your business, you will add income, period.

So, consider the following questions:

What more can you do to REACH out?   Brainstorm here.

How can you improve your RESPONSE so it's efficient, enjoyable and profitable?

How can you streamline your relationship building technique to reach more people in less time?

CHAPTER 8
Nagging Your Way to Success

Are you a little shy of marketing, especially through repeat emails or calls? It's called 'being a loving nag' and we know you have what it takes – especially if you're a parent, or have ever been a child.

8

Wisdom Nugget:

Do you have children or a husband or wife? To get the impact of this wisdom nugget, picture in your mind a significant person – or even pet - in your life.

When was the last time you asked that person to do something and it took several 'reminder-ings' to get satisfaction?

Maybe you asked them to, 'get your boots on or you'll be late for school.'

Or, 'the faucet is still leaking honey, would you have a look and see if we need to call a plumber?'

If you're a dog lover like us, you may be quite familiar with a request that sounds something like this: 'Sit. Siiiit. Rover, sit! Come and sit. SIT! Good boy!'

Now for the million-dollar question: How many times did you have to ask, before you got what you wanted?

If you said 5, 6, or even 7 times, you are not alone. And because you know how this feels, you're going to be great at translating this skill into your business.

We call it the 'Art of Being a Loving Nag'. And if you put your heart into it for the benefit of your business, you can create 5, 6, and even 7 figure results – no exaggeration.

CASE STUDY:

We were working with John Conaway[1] to promote a series of teleconferences for network marketers the other day. There were two dates for these free calls, and after sending out the announcement for the first, about 30 people signed up. Of those, about 20 attended the conference, and just one person purchased the training program that was offered on the call.

For the second date, we wanted to generate a much deeper result. Obviously the goal was to increase signups to the teleconference so that more people came to the call. Here is what we did.

1. In addition to the first announcement, we sent a second invitation one day before the actual day of the call. The main message in it was, 'Can you join us tomorrow?'

This simple second reminder added over 75 people to the call roster…an increase of over 200%.

2. Each individual who signed up for the call also got a reminder – this time to attend the call. Just because they were signed up was no guarantee they would show up.

    About 50 people attended the call.

3. After the conference was over, a reminder of the program offer was sent out, and 4 people purchased.

4. If we wanted to be even more loving with our nagging, we might send another reminder before the program starts – 'Last chance to become part of the Savvy Sponsoring Program this month.'

CASE STUDY:

My Ping Pong club – the Calgary United Senior Table Tennis Association, CUSSTA for short - recently held their Annual General Meeting. As with many recreational clubs, the meeting coincided with one of their biggest money-making events, a silent auction.

All members received the minutes a week before, in the form of a 12 page, double-sided tome. "How on earth," thought I, "will they get ANYone to attend?"

Of course, they did. I was really quite impressed. They lovingly nagged me by mail, by phone, in person, the week prior when I went into the club, and again by phone. Each time, the reminder came with another reason it would benefit me to attend – there would be refreshments; practice time would be no charge that day; member ID cards would be distributed with our new photos.

In the end, I counted over 60 in attendance and the silent auction appeared a success – the club's financial well-being looked assured for another year.

All of this occurred on a sunny Saturday afternoon that felt a little like spring in Calgary. Amazing, the difference a little nagging can make.

You can replicate this kind of result by wrapping your head around the benefit – to your business AND to your clients – of being a loving nag. In fact, you can apply the loving nag theory to any promotion you do in your business.

Even if you're shy, just thinking about following through as the art of lovingly nagging could be the breakthrough you're looking for.

Start brainstorming here about how you can profitably - and perhaps even enjoyably - be a 'loving nag' in your business:

REVIEW AND RECAP: MONEY

You've been reading this book because you're looking for something. Let's pause for a moment here and check to see if you've found it.

Review and Recap

We've come to the end of the 'Money' section in this book. In each of the foregoing chapters, we've shared an important concept that if you apply, will bring income into your business.

1. **Create one or more Pink Spoon offerings** for your business, so people can try a free sample of what you offer. Make it possible – at every juncture – for your clients to try you before they buy you.

2. **Watch and listen – acutely – for the desire lines** your clients leave, so you can sell them what they want. There are things your clients want to buy from you, that you aren't selling them yet.

3. **Build a Multiple Streams Funnel.** Design you business so clients and money flow naturally through to you.

4. **Ask, "What's the fastest path to money?"** There is money your clients would spend with you right now, if they understood how.

5. **Get Permission to keep in touch.** You won't always get a 'kiss' on the first date. So make sure you get a phone number or email address for next time!

6. **Clean up your communication.** One thing at a time – one-banana - in every advertisement, promotion or website. A confused mind always says no, so stop confusing.

7. **Create conversations that cause a response.** The emphasis is on deepening relationships – lots of them – in a way that's sustainable for you. The more you can perfect this, the more business will flow to you.

8. **Learn to love being a nag.** You do it in other parts of your life, so you can do it in your business. Especially if it means your clients – and your bottom line - are happy, right?

Now let's tie it all together in the last two chapters in this section, beginning with the one we call 'Mad Science.'

CHAPTER 9
Mad Science

Do you know your numbers? Sales, expenses, the hours you work? How about how much you'd like to earn this year? If you said 'no,' you're not alone, but not for long…

9

One of the more surprising things we've learned over the years is this:

The act of measuring the growth of your business is a very large contributor to actual growth.

Put another way? If you want to grow your business, don't just try to grow it. Measure it. Because measuring will make it grow too.

An extension of this understanding is what we've come to consider a fact:

Most new business owners balk at measuring. The ones that stick around are the ones that grow from balking to accepting and then to relishing the measuring process. It's a sort of barometer of the owner's commitment to being around in the long term.

The cheeky way to put it is this: Hobbyists (business owners for whom their business is really just a hobby) resist the idea of measuring. It's too serious a thing to do for it to fit into their worldview of how running a business should feel.

Ignorance is not bliss... you need to know what your business is doing in order to create success. Many new business owners fit into the hobby category because their commitment hasn't yet been tested.

Business owners who have really started to dig into the idea of a long-term abundant livelihood – and get past the initial honeymoon stage of being in business - measure.

The corollary of this? If you find yourself resisting the idea of measuring, ask yourself if you want to be in business 10 years from now. Then ask in what way you'd like to be in business 10 years from now – in the same place you're in now, or further along, earning more and enjoying more?

Here's the good news. With a little help, measuring does not have to be hard. With a little help[1], it can actually be fun in a mad scientist kind of way.

One person even described it as a little like rewarding her dog with a treat when he did a trick. If she did something right in her business, her numbers would show it. That's the reward of measuring – you know when you get it right.

So, here's the quick and dirty version of 7 things we recommend you measure in your business each week. If each week seems too big a leap for now, go with each month:

1. **The number of people** in your customer databank, or your newsletter subscriber list. Or any other 'group' of people you keep track of that's pertinent.

2. **The number of things** you are selling them, including their price points. Do you have 3 core services? Or 1 core service and 5 complementary products? Maybe you have 100 products in your store. Keep track. When you add or take away, make note.

3. **How much of each thing** you are selling. Did you sell 100 of widget A and get 3 returns of widget B? Have you had 10 new clients each week for three months and then all of a sudden 23? Quick, what did you do, and how will you repeat it?

4. **How many times** do you communicate directly with your current clients, and with what promotional offer? Did you send out a coupon to 25 of your best clients this week? Good, mark it down.

5. **How much money** do you want to earn this year? What does that break out to per month?

6. **How much money** did you earn this week and is that going to add up to your goal for the year?

7. **How much money** do you spend in your business each

week, and what can you reduce? If you choose not to reduce your spending right now, what could you, if you had to?

Of course, just measuring isn't where the exciting part comes in. Figuring out what the numbers tell you is. So as you build your data, stretch yourself with just two basic questions:

"What worked this week and do I want to do more of it?"

"What isn't working and should I stop doing it right away? If not, how do I improve it and try again?"

That's really it when it comes to an overview about Mad Science.

Wisdom Nugget:

When you're in business for yourself, it is enormously easy to get caught up in money. Getting caught up in money is another way of saying getting caught up in working harder, putting in longer hours, and just generally going crazy over your business.

Going crazy over your business is not – not ever – a pretty sight. The good news is you have a choice. You don't ever have to be in a position to wonder and get caught up with money, putting yourself in danger of going crazy with it.

Simply put: measuring is the antidote to business craziness. And having had our share of the crazies, this is why we've included this chapter.

What follows is something we call 'The Money Game' - a fun place to start measuring. This simple tool has now been used by thousands of business owners around the world.

The thing is, it's such a simple game, it often comes across as mundane, and many people skip it. They figure they 'get' it, and they don't need to 'do' it.

While you can 'get' the concept of the Money Game intellectually, there is something about going through the process of doing it that we're inviting you to feel.

If you're open to it, you'll find your Money Game gives you benchmarks that serve as a lighthouse or North Star. You'll be able to keep steering in the right direction because of it.

So get out a pencil and a calculator, and as we go through it, play along.

CHAPTER 10
The Money Game

As your plans and energy towards your business ebb and flow as they naturally will, part of the beauty of playing the Money Game is that you'll be ready to adjust.

10

This involves some basic math. Really!

At the top of a blank piece of paper, write the words 'My Money Game' and make a note of the date.

For the purposes of this exercise, decide on a figure that we'll call your financial goals for the next 12 months. Write this on the first line:

My goal for the business is to earn $ _____ in the next 12 months.

Note, it doesn't matter if your goal is $100,000, $10,000, $10 million or $100 million. There's no right or wrong answer.

You'll be revisiting and refining the worksheet numerous times a year, so don't worry about getting it 'precisely right.'

Now sit back for a moment, and consider your financial goal for the next 12 months.

If we take the figure $120,000 as an example, thinking about building your business may feel pretty daunting.

But when you break down a single large financial goal into chunks, things instantly become more achievable and your chances of success are immediately much higher.

So consider this:

If 100 people pay you $100 each month for something, that's $10,000 per month or $120,000 over the course of the year.

But maybe you don't sell anything – yet – for $100 a month. Alright, try this on for size:

If 100 people pay $39, that's $3900 per month or $46,800 over the course of the year.

If your one-year financial goal happens to be $150,000, then…you got it. You need to settle on three things to sell at $39 apiece, and sell 100 of these products or services each month in order to reach $150,000 for that year.

Not too bad.

Based on the size of your current newsletter list, customer databank, or existing customer list, if 50 seems like a more reasonable number than 100, simply substitute the numbers.

Let's try it.

If 50 (as compared with 100) people pay $39 per month, that's $1,950 each month or $23,400 over the course of the year.

NOTE: This is where the aspect of the money game comes in and powerfully shifts us into a bigger picture perspective.

When forecasting the revenue for your business using the Money Game...you can use a slide rule for each of the pertinent numbers.

And for each of the numbers, you can experiment with putting in the numbers you are most comfortable with.

So whether it's the number of people you project, anticipate or research tells you can scientifically expect to buy your product, OR - Whether it's the price tag that you would be comfortable pricing your material at,

you can shift those numbers up and down and until you end with a monthly gross revenue number as well as a yearly number that fits into the bigger picture of your yearly financial goals.

This may mean that you have 5 revenue streams, or 15. Or it could mean that you only have 3. Try it and see what you come up with, because the real magic of the Money Game is when you extrapolate it and personalize it.

Now, if we take the last statement...

If 50 people pay $39 each month, that equals $23,400 each year.

If you can reasonably offer 6 in-demand products or services at that rate...voila. You have yourself $150,000 for that year.

Does this example help highlight how very doable that is?

It's about more than the mechanics of the math. It's a way for you to reframe the way you look at earning income.

Enjoy playing with the Money Game.

Just remember that it is a game that works, and that if you're willing to reframe your mind around this way of looking at things, it can make a business owner's life a lot different on a day-to-day basis. That's you!

Ready to extrapolate to your situation?

What are your financial targets and how can you break them down so that you reach your yearly goal? Play around with the numbers and see what happens.

Remember the Multiple Streams Funnel that we talked about in Chapter 3? Start to fill in various products/services that you can offer in each level based on your Money Game numbers.

MEANING

"Your work is to discover your work and then with all your heart to give yourself to it."

Buddha

CHAPTER 11
Gravy Pans

Got tons to do, and not enough time? Just like how gravy gets made as a byproduct of roasting a chicken – you're getting more done than you think.

11

'Not enough.'

These two little words are never more frequently used than with regards to time.

And it's never more apparent when you're a business owner. Stop for a moment and take stock. How are you with time, right now? Got lots? Or are you on the run?

If you said the latter, you've definitely got company. Ask around among your business owner friends and you'll find it's a common theme. Everyone's got tons to do and not enough time.

So here's the thing. How about we get things rolling with a question:

How can you get more done in less time?

We ask this not because there's a magic pill that makes it possible to stretch the days or the hours. But by asking this question we can start shedding some light on a few things.

In fact, while we're at it, why don't we ask a more challenging question – one that at first glance might seem outlandish:

How can you get 10 times the result with half the amount of effort?

Even though it may be hard, take the question seriously for a moment. Try asking it again, only this time with the attitude that you have the power to answer it, in all reasonableness.

How can you get 10 times the result with half the amount of effort?

It seems paradoxical, but the very act of asking an outlandish question like this can open us up to new possibilities. In this case, we begin to sense that somewhere, there may be a path that we haven't discovered yet. One that allows us to get more of what we want, whether that be more time, results, meaning, money or something else entirely.

One thing we seem to know for sure is the path is very likely NOT a straight line. There's no logical progression from point A through point Z.

No, there's a less linear way of looking at the issue of getting more done in less time.

The invitation here is this:

Reconsider how you can do more with what you're already doing. And in doing so, recognize you're getting a lot more done than you think.

"I beg your pardon?"

Yes, it seems odd, but relax a moment and see what happens. Relaxed is the best state to be in if you're going to try and transform an old way of thinking.

The thing is, getting more results with less effort doesn't have to be hard. Here's an example. Let's say you're roasting a chicken; one of those wonderful activities that shines a light on things that matter: a great meal, conversation, laughter and family.

While you're roasting a chicken…what else can you think is happening inside the oven?

If you said gravy's getting made, you're right. When you're roasting a chicken, even though you're not making any extra effort, you're also making gravy by catching the drippings in a pan.

But – this is true only if you recognize the value of the gravy. (Some people miss this, and throw out great gravy, right? That's because they're so single-mindedly focused on roasting chicken.)

With this example in mind, let's try the invitation again.

What if you are already getting a lot more done than you think?

This isn't just a fancy way of describing multitasking either. It's actually a shift in the way you look at what can be considered productive activity in your business.

What are some ordinary activities you do in your business, that bring with them unexpected 'gravy'?

How can you create more results with the same (or less) amount of effort?

As a leading business owner in your field, you might think, "I have to find time to write my book." The unexpected truth may be that you're already writing a book when you write an article once a month. Maybe you've already finished one.

The articles are the chicken; the book is the gravy. Got it?

(Hint: This is in large part how we wrote this book.)

Wisdom nugget:

Are you someone who chronically wishes you had more time, so you could get more done?

Chapter 11: Gravy Pans   133

How would it feel to consider you're getting much more done than you think, but that you need to look at what you're doing with a different set of glasses, to realize just how much you're getting done?

Instead of rushing around trying to fit more 'doing' into your day, what possibilities would arise if you let yourself 'be' with what you're already doing…and put it all to best use?

After all, you wouldn't throw out good drippings from roasting a chicken would you? Why throw away the results that are already all around?

Make sure you start looking for where the unexpected extra results are being created in your business and life, and then make gravy.

CASE STUDY:

Ironically for a chapter on making gravy, the restaurant industry makes a great case study.

Restaurants, like many other retail service businesses, often come face to face with the challenge of how to make more money with the same amount of resources and time.

The answer for this particular service industry is actually quite straightforward. Restaurants seeking additional income with little to no additional expense, should give serious consideration to doing catering as an income stream.

Think about it. The same kitchen staff, equipment and menu can accommodate a significant number of catering orders in the down time of a regular day.

It's only a question of whether a restaurant can see itself in a different light, and stop throwing away the proverbial 'gravy.'

CASE STUDY:

Herb, Bud and the Beanstalk Boys is a greenhouse operation run by 5 partners as part of a funding initiative in the province of Alberta.[1] In it, adults with disabilities become active in their lives through the running of a small business.

In their first year, the Beanstalk Boys successfully sold a small amount of fresh vegetables at the end of the growing season. Having seen positive cash flow, it was a good year.

Part way through their second year at the time of writing this book, the business has already doubled their income, as a result of selling seedlings.

> Along the way to growing vegetables, are seedlings, and though vegetables will still be on offer in a few months, the seedlings – which they'd been growing all along - have already stolen the season.

Along the path to creating what matters to you in your life, look closely at your business. We're confident you'll discover there are pools of gravy all around you that you only need scoop up and serve.

Doing more with less time really doesn't have to be hard. Just remember the Gravy Pan.

"When faced with two insoluble problems, try tackling both at once."

- International economic forecaster Linda Starke[2]

Wisdom nugget:

How can you make the most of your current business activities? Where is there opportunity to create more with less?

Last but not least, as with all the side door concepts in Money, Meaning & Beyond, the 'Gravy Pan' can be applied to your life, not just your business.

What are some of the ordinary things you do in your life that create unexpected added results? How can you make gravy from them?

CHAPTER 12
No Great Thing is Accomplished Alone

*Together we know everything and everyone,
and can do everything we're meant to do.
So learn to give first, and you will receive.*

12

Wisdom Nugget:

A man is granted permission to see both heaven and hell while he is still alive. First he goes to visit hell. He goes down, opens up this big door, and sees a huge banquet hall. There's a long table in the center of the room, with people seated on both sides. The table is laden with every imaginable delicacy: crisp roast suckling pig, apricot-glazed goose, candied yams, butter-drenched green beans, piping-hot bread spread with fragrant jam, warm pies topped with Ben & Jerry's ice cream.

As he's looking at this scene the man sees that the people seated at the table are crying and wailing and in terrible pain. He looks a little closer and sees that the utensils the people have to eat with have such long handles that it's impossible for them to get the food into their mouths.

Depressed, with a heavy heart, the man goes to visit heaven. He opens the door and sees virtually the same huge banquet room – the same long table covered with

> the same delicious food, and people sitting on both sides of the table with the same long-handled utensils.
>
> But instead of crying in pain and hunger, these people are laughing, singing and rejoicing. The man looks closer and sees that the people in heaven, instead of trying to feed only themselves, are feeding one another.

-Ancient Eastern Parable[1]

There is no more effective way to build your business than to help and be helped, just like the people in our parable.

In the language of business, this is often called a joint venture. So first and foremost, what is a joint venture?

Simply put, a joint venture is when two or more business owners collaborate in a way that benefits all the businesses involved, as well as their clients.

For example, if a graphic design business were to pursue a joint venture with a printing business, we can readily see both businesses increasing their income as a result.

How about when a weight loss business joint ventures with a health club owner? Could we envision a better result for the clients of both businesses?

The examples are everywhere, when you start to look. Especially in the online world, as you embrace Pink Spoon Marketing™ and the multiple streams funnel, you'll discover that it can be lucrative and enjoyable to joint venture more often.

One of the easiest ways to begin doing more joint ventures is by using the Internet. Let's say you've followed the steps in Chapter 5, and augmented your income-generating abilities by building an email database of clients and prospects.

You now have what's called a 'permission asset' or list of people you can communicate with. This immediately opens up doors to more quality collaboration – allowing you to work closely with people you might never have the chance to, in the offline world.

CASE STUDY:

ANDREA

Many long years ago – okay only five – I decided to start building a list. I'd heard so many people talk about building a list as an important thing to do because it would lead to business and life opportunities – it seemed too good to be true, so I wanted to try it for myself.

I decided to write some articles about 'How to Help the Planet and Enjoy Life at the Same Time' and called the project 'Joy to the Planet'[2] It was my way of taking some of the things I do in my life and sharing them with others – hopefully in a helpful way, and it ends up with a pretty special story.

> You've probably heard of a young woman named Julia Butterfly-Hill. She's the one who spent 738 days, 180 feet up in the branches of a 1000 year-old Redwood tree she called Luna, and is now founder of an organization called Circle of Life.[3]
>
> As a result of building the Joy to the Planet list of readers to over 5,000, I had the nerve one day to write to Julia and ask if she'd be willing to be interviewed by phone on the record, about what was 'new' in her life. Not only because of my charm, I'm sure, she agreed, and a really delightful 30-minute audio is the result.
>
> By giving me her time, I've been able to make this audio recording available to hundreds and soon thousands of people to hear – something that benefits her cause, my project and the people who listen to the recording. All because we decided to do something together, in a mini joint venture.

Who could you interview, joint venture, or collaborate with, to the benefit of your business and your clients? It could be as simple as an interview as in our case study, or it could be as complicated as holding a charity event together.

How can you go about making this kind of thing happen?

Well, there's more than one route to success. But what we'd really like to highlight is the 'give and you shall receive' strategy.

To set the scene a bit, and give you a head start, let's not hold the ugly truth back. Many, many people – especially online – try to joint venture in a very crude way without any foreplay. They simply send an email to the person they've targeted, saying, "Hey, will you promote my product/service/program/business?" Or, even worse, "I think we should do something together? What do you think we should do?"

To which our reply is usually, "Who the heck are you and why would we want to do something with you?" Actually no, we're a little more polite than that, but you take our point.

So if the goal is to do more things together, what's the problem with this scenario? Hint: It's something to do with giving first, and then receiving.

Whether it's online or off, when approaching a joint venture, always ask the question: What's in it for your potential joint venture partner?

Emails like the above usually end up deleted because they are all about the person sending it, not about a mutual benefit. If there is nothing in it for them, there is no reason for them to consider your request.

Wisdom nugget:

We live in a world of give and take; a world of checks and balances. When something is out of balance, nature adapts and adjusts so it can return to a state of equilibrium. The same thing applies in business. By leading with an offer to give, you are naturally paving the way for something to be given in return.

Give it some thought and note that you may find your thought process shifting as you do.

Here are a few key points to bear in mind when exploring collaborative opportunities:

- Select your partners with care. The main criteria is that the partner should be someone who is already in touch with, or doing business with, people you want to do business with too. And they should also be someone you would actually want to share or cross-promote to your own list.

  Don't ask them to help you if you aren't ready to say yes when they ask you back.

- Get to know these potential partners before jumping into a big collaborative project. In preparation for approaching them with an invitation, sign up for their publications, visit their websites, read everything about them and their history where possible. Try to understand their values and motivation as best you can from what they make public.

- Start asking your self, "What value could I provide this partner? What do I have that they don't? What could they be doing that they aren't? What challenge or goals are they pursuing and how can I help them get there?"

Important: If you're having difficulty finding something you could help your potential partner with, keep looking. They aren't the best match for you right now.

Once you've narrowed down your list to one or two potential partners, it's time to finesse the approach. Remember finding joint venture partners is not an automated, mass campaign. Truly great collaborations can lead to lifelong partnerships and will take root only with a customized, heart-centered approach, and do take time to build.

What you may not realize yet is that most people in business – especially those who do some work online - will usually be open to discussing a new business-building possibility for at least five minutes. Just make sure you heed the golden rule of joint ventures and use that five minutes wisely.

Give first and you shall receive.

Ask, "what's in it for them?" Make it easy for them to say yes. Focus on the benefits to them, and allow them to get to know you over time. A great collaboration can be the result, no matter how 'successful' or out-of-reach you think they are.

Wisdom nugget:

Think of three people you would LOVE to joint venture with, sky's the limit. What could you offer them? Don't be afraid to get a little creative, it may not be something obvious...

What is your biggest fear about using a collaborative approach to your business?

Remember – doing things together is one of the most underplayed and most enjoyable business strategies in existence. Be willing to be honest with yourself about your fears, so you can begin to excavate your inner roadblocks.

Where else could the 'give and you shall receive' strategy serve you in your business? Or in your life?

CHAPTER 13
Picking the Ripe Apples

Are you too smart for your own good? Stop making things complicated for yourself. It all starts with picking the ripe apples.

13

Imagine yourself in an apple orchard for a moment. Picture yourself reaching your arm out, fingers curving around the bottom of an apple.

You pull.

But instead of the apple falling into your hand, the entire branch comes with it.

When an apple isn't quite ripe, it sticks to its branch.

On the other hand, when it's ripe, it quietly breaks away from its branch with a snick.

There's something to learn from the way a ripe apple effortlessly leaves its tree when it's time.[1]

As business owners, one of the valuable things to learn is that there is a season for everything. And sometimes, in our single-minded focus to get 'something' done, we force that 'something' before it's time.

The result? Not much to show for a lot of effort!

If you've been trying to get something done…

Or you've been trying to convince someone of something…

Or if you think you simply must persist towards a certain goal or target or result…

Ask yourself…is this an apple that's not quite ripe, and must I pick this particular apple now?

The answer is usually no, there are other apples – or even other fruit - that are ripe right now that would be less difficult to pick.

Often, bright people can think their way into a decision that's based on logic alone. Their intellect 'informs' them that their choice is the smart one.

But recognizing there is a natural cycle to everything – including business – will help you put your effort where it's warranted…where the ripe apples are.

Chapter 13: Picking the Ripe Apples

Wisdom Nugget:

Struggle – of all kinds, in business and life – is highly over-rated. Are you someone who thinks you have to struggle or work hard in order to achieve something? Where did you learn this message?

Wo / wor sind die reifen Äpfel?
Won / wen kann ich mühelos pflücken?
Won / wen sollte ich lieber noch etwas pflegen?

Consider the possibility that you could achieve just as much if not more, in your life, not by struggling, but with ease. What feelings come up for you when you explore this concept?

Freely brainstorm and list what you are struggling with right now, using this space:

On the above list, what are three things you could let go of, and stop struggling? Put a line through each of those. Take just a moment longer here and become aware of your energy and emotions. How do you feel as a result of shedding just a little of your habit of struggling?

CHAPTER 14
Excuse Me, Will you Be My Google?

*Want an easy business-building strategy for a change?
Like Disc Jockeys of another era, your clients are
looking to you to be their filter.*

14

Do you remember when radio disc jockeys used to be trusted friends?

Whenever they recommended a new recording artist, you would listen and often purchase that CD or cassette?

Whether you realized it or not, that disc jockey was a filter for you - someone you trusted to tell you what to pay attention to.

In a very real way, that's what we as enlightened business owners are becoming for our clients. Why?

Human filters of this kind are becoming increasingly in demand.

The fact is people are no longer looking for more information. They're looking for the perfect piece of information at the precise moment they want it. For the most part, they're busy, overwhelmed, and just trying to make sense of their world.

And they're looking for people they trust to find it. In every field of business, they're looking for people they can look to, to make their life meaningful.

What should I read?

Who should I observe?

What business models work?

How should I dress, decorate, entertain?

Which artists are important? What charities are worthwhile? Which doctor should I see? Should I take that person to court?

Whether you're a wedding planner or a mortgage broker, if you're doing a good job in your business, people are already asking you for your opinion.

As a business owner, you have a real opportunity to become a trusted resource for your clients through whatever product or service you offer. At its best, business becomes more than a transaction.

And that's when you successfully leap from 'being in business' to 'being in a business that matters.' Businesses that matter elevate the lives of the people around them.

Chapter 14: Excuse Me, Will You Be My Google?

So consider becoming a Google[1] for your clients. Don't just give them information. Give them the right information, filtered for them, and along the way, be sure to tell them what you're doing. This helps them build the trust bond and increases your value to them.

It's no coincidence that life is imitating technology in this way.

In the online world where there are so many billions of pieces of information, who has reigned supreme?

Answer: search engines like Google that make sense of the information and that filter the information. In fact, the ability to get an answer to any question at any given moment each day has led some people to speculate that Google has become a little like God.[2]

In future, we believe increasing numbers of leading business owners will find value in becoming human Googles for their clients. Human browsers.

As you go about serving your clients and delivering solutions to their problems, remember… your highest and best value to your client is in filtering the solutions that are perfect for them.

Think of yourself as a human browser. Begin positioning yourself as such.

Not only does it make it easier to deliver value just by being you, but it's exactly what your clients want from you.

Simple.

Wisdom nugget:

What do you read? Why do you read it? Would your clients value knowing this? How can you share this filtered information with them?

Chapter 14: Excuse Me, Will You Be My Google?

Who do you turn to for answers on various topics? Who are your Googles and why do you trust them? What can you learn by putting the shoe on the other foot?

Begin taking note of when your clients ask you for your opinion. What questions are you getting most often? Is it possible many more of your clients are wondering the same thing? How can you provide the answer to these questions on a larger scale?

CHAPTER 15
The Lone Ranger Syndrome

Is your brain about to burst from all the little details? The right help at the right price will clear your head and rekindle the pleasure of being in business.

15

It's not unusual for either of us to get variations of this question:

> "Tina, I want to build my website, set up some Pink Spoons and manage my different streams of income, including online. So how do I become tech-savvy?"

Our response: "Why should you become tech-savvy?"

It's easy when adding online elements to our business to think that we need to do it all ourselves, which simply isn't true...

As a small business owner, isn't your time better spent elsewhere, such as delivering value to your clients or building your business? When your time is limited, doesn't it make sense to work on the stuff that only YOU can do in your business?

It's a pet peeve of ours to see people waste their time and effort learning skills that are a poor match to their talents, they don't enjoy, and in many cases don't benefit their business!

So why is this so common? Most people think they can't afford to hire help for themselves and their business, especially in the early days when cash flow may be tight. And so they resign themselves to either:

- Doing everything themselves and letting their business suffer, OR

- Under-utilizing the help that they do have, thus hampering their growth.

On behalf of your sanity and the growth of your business, hire some help sooner rather than later.[1]

One of the best resources for support available these days is to hire a Virtual Assistant. Also known as a VA, these skilled professionals are able to help with anything from general administrative tasks, customer service, technical projects, marketing initiatives and more. The word Virtual simply refers to the fact that they work from their location, not yours, and that may mean they're up to half way around the globe.

Because VAs usually work as contractors, you can hire them[2] for as much or as little work as you need, be it just a few hours each week or up to full time hours as your business grows. Since VAs work from home and have their own equipment, you save the cost of hiring and housing a fulltime local assistant.

But won't a VA – or any other kind of help for that matter – cost money? Money that you may not feel you can spare just now? The answer is yes, however there is one key point about turning a VA from a business liability, into a true asset.

Think of them as a Profit Center.

Instead of an expense, like stationary, office furniture, or your internet connection, a Virtual Assistant can be a profit center.

Most people don't think about 'getting help' this way, so it's to your benefit if you do. By focusing your VA on profit generating tasks, you leverage yourself, add capacity to your business and in fact, alleviate the pressure on you to be the only 'bread winner' in the business – a very common situation if you're working solo.

Although it seems simple on the outside, this one mind-set shift will differentiate you from other business owners if you go ahead and implement it.

Ask, "How Can My Virtual Assistant Be a Profit Center In My Company?"

This mindset-shift is one of the main reasons why we have been able to help build our client companies so quickly from six figures to seven. Think about it. Being able to add capacity in a way that makes it possible for you to do much more work, more quickly, is a pretty neat thing. Not to mention bringing in more money!

Let's talk a bit more about what these profit-generating tasks might be. First, the best VAs are NOT just glorified secretaries.

Particularly in the online world, there are dozens of things a VA can do that a 'real-world' secretary cannot. Here are just few real-world examples you can put into practice right away.

1. Have Your Virtual Assistant Help Actively Build Your Reservoir of Customers.

In an online world, we all know it to be true, if you aren't collecting email addresses from your website visitors, you are just not going to make it.

Building a reservoir of newsletter readers, ezine subscribers or readers of your autoresponders is one of the most important, yet often overlooked responsibilities of an online business owner.

Yet...building this list can sometimes be a routine task, a perfect candidate to delegate to a Virtual Assistant. The more email addresses you have in your database, the more potential sales you'll be able to make. So it follows that by assigning your VA the task of consistently and assertively building this list… you will grow your bottom line.

2. Have Your Virtual Assistant Help Cultivate Strong Affiliate Relationships

Do you have an affiliate referral program for your online products and services? As you may know, an affiliate program can be a powerful element in the success of an online business.

Using the technology available in most 'shopping cart' systems, you can keep track of people who recommend your items for sale to their readers.

The sales that occur as a result of these affiliates can be significant. But most online businesses, perhaps including yours, are not making full use of their affiliate program. Sales opportunities get missed because you haven't taken the time and effort to cultivate strong affiliates.

Enter your Virtual Assistant. By putting your VA 'in charge' of your affiliate program, you ensure that your affiliates get every problem solved, every need met, and feel like real VIPs.

Over the long term, this is one of the most outstanding pieces of small business work that you can hand over to your VA.

Read our lips. Having your VA help cultivate your affiliate team MEANS MONEY. Might you be ready to appoint your VA your official 'Manager of Ensuring Your Affiliate Team is Happy?'

3. Have Your Virtual Assistant Manage your Newsletter

From our discussion in Chapter 5, you understand clearly the importance of keeping in regular touch with your list, which can be a challenge at times.

Assign your VA the task of managing your newsletter. They can take care of researching newsletter topics, formatting, and broadcasting issues. As they become more familiar with your writing style and general content, they may be able to help draft the newsletter on your behalf.

So what else could a VA be doing for you?

Some business owners find it tough to decide what to delegate to their VA. This is especially true for those of us who find it hard to let go of control (come on, we're sure that's you on some days!)

If you are unsure where you could use the help, try asking yourself these simple questions throughout your business day:

"Is this something that a VA could do for me? What, exactly, are the little details that are making my head feel like it's going to burst? Is this the best use of my time?

Does this task belong in my 'yuck' bucket? How great would it be to hand over a 'yuck bucket' of tasks to a trusted helper? And how much more money could I earn for the business if I weren't slogging through the details?"

Remember that you want to be able to focus your own efforts on those things that *only you can do for your business*. Anything else is fair game for your Virtual Assistant's 'To Do' list.

CASE STUDY:

In a conversation with Jillian Middleton[3] – Head Coach of Savvy Sponsoring - we discovered she was still doing a lot of administrative work for her coaching business. Specifically, her program participants were faxing their coaching agreements to her, which she would then forward to her assistant.

When I asked her why she was the one taking care of these details, she said "I'm not sure exactly, we've just always done it this way". We both agreed this wasn't the best use of her time, and found a solution that bypassed her.[4]

Even though the amount of time saved was actually relatively small, Jillian was thrilled to "get the details out of her head" and free up energy for more strategic things.

Little things can make a big difference, especially if we don't enjoy doing them!

What 'busy work' tasks do you find yourself doing throughout the day? Pay attention to things you do when you should be focused on marketing and growth activities. These are especially ripe for delegation.

CASE STUDY:

Here's a different example of how you can utilize an assistant to create bottom-line results:

We recently heard from a former client who had taken the step of hiring a bookkeeper for her business. But the interesting thing is – she didn't hire the bookkeeper because she hates bookkeeping. In fact, she actually really enjoys it! And that's exactly why she had to stop doing it. Instead of doing her business-building activities, she'd get into the time-sucking habit of doing it herself for fun.

Not wanting this to be a temptation any longer, she outsourced this task and reclaimed her time for things more deserving of her attention. It goes to

> show that sometimes busy work can come in the form of something you enjoy.

What are the most pressing tasks in your business that you wish you could "just get done?" Begin a list here.

CHAPTER 16
Salad Bowls

Too tired all the time for this to be sustainable?
When whisking a salad dressing, a good bowl
makes all the difference to your wrist.
Who (and what) are you leaning on?

16

Like you, one of things that matters most to us is our families. As you'll read in this chapter, some of the greatest business metaphors can come out of the blue, when we're spending quality time with our loved ones.

A story from Andrea:

> I'm not the world's greatest cook, by far. But my husband Mike tells me I'm getting better.
>
> A lot of the time I think I found cooking 'just boring.' But recently something happened in the kitchen that made me realize, there is a lot more going on sometimes than just food preparation!
>
> One of Mike's favorites for dinner is a homemade Caesar Salad. Not your store-bought Caesar Salad dressing mind you, but made from scratch.
>
> And actually I've gotten the hang of it over the years, which is nice. Even though it's not perfectly consistent each time, I know what it takes and can usually produce something quite nice.

The other day though, while I was whisking the dressing in a bowl, Mike came up behind me and gave me a hug. My mind was pretty much elsewhere, probably thinking about a client situation or something, but when he came up behind me I snapped back to the present.

He put his chin on my head and just hung out for a bit, while I continued to whisk. After a minute he said, "Andrea, how come you're whisking like that?"

To which I replied, "Like what?"

His reply…"That." And took my hand.

Now you need to know that Mike's been trained as a professional chef. So it's a pretty big deal for me to be cooking anything in his presence and pass muster. So when he grabbed my hand, I let my arm go limp and followed his lead.

He proceeded to whisk, with my hand under his, with much more energy than I had been before, but his arm was loose and he was making a lot of noise.

Sure enough, after just a quick half minute, the dressing had gelled, smooth like silk and no funny lumps.

What was the difference? It took me a moment to register it, but when I did, it was pretty obvious.

Mike's whisking banged up against the walls of the bowl, in big circles. Almost as though we weren't *whisking the dressing in the middle of the bowl, but brushing up against the sides of it.*

Funny thing, the whisking was a lot easier too, because the bowl was doing the work.

By contrast, my small circular wrist motions tended to be in the middle of the bowl, and I was much more quiet about it. Almost as if the edge of the bowl was made of something breakable and I mustn't get it dirty.

Life and business, I realized in that moment, have something in common with making salad dressing! In our lives, we have every opportunity to lean up against the environment we're in, and in so doing, relax our effort, conserve our energy and do a great job.

Rather than work harder to get results, we can get better results with less effort, if we set ourselves up to lean on our favorite people and things.[1]

Wisdom nugget:

A pad of paper and pen at a favorite desk could be the perfect physical environment for a writer to access their deepest work.

A regular subscription to three industry magazines could be the right intellectual environment for a financial advisor to succeed.

Can you imagine how a mastermind group could be just the kind of emotional support for a first-time business owner in any field?

How about an online membership or office assistant as an accountability environment? Some business owners get a lot out of having a mentor as a spiritual environment.

As you can see, there are many types of environments that you live and work in everyday. Are these environments serving you and lifting you up? Which ones can you identify as draining your energy, and how can you get rid of them?

In what way can you elevate your support environment this month? Brainstorm at least five possible things you could do, from de-cluttering your office space to buying a glorious piece of art, or any of the above.

CHAPTER 17
The Clay is Never Dry

Can't seem to get started? Trapped in procrastination?
Focus on completion, not perfection.

17

A realtor friend[1] once told us, "There is no such thing as a mistake in Real Estate." Meaning that, if you feel as though you've made a mistake in Real Estate, you only have to wait long enough, and it will turn out alright – your mistake will no longer seem like a mistake.

We're of an opinion that's a little more extreme, that is – 'There is no such thing as a mistake.' Everything is fixable, absolutely everything.

Put another way – a metaphysical kind of way – we like how Abraham-Hicks[2] puts it, that is, "The Clay is Never Dry." If we think of our businesses as works of art, or sculptures in progress – just for a moment – we can tap into a feeling of great freedom. We can start to understand there's never a time when we can't go back and mold, shape or refine.

Consider that phrase for a moment and see whether it releases you from some of the pressures of being perfect.

CASE STUDY:

I was training a Virtual Assistant for one of my clients a little while ago.

I was showing her around a few systems, and noticed when it was her turn, she would come back a few times to make sure that she was 'doing it right'.

While there's nothing wrong with wanting to 'do things right the first time,' I could feel the enormous amount of pressure it was causing her.

It occurred to me how much easier it would be, to come from a place of knowing 'It's all fixable.' Get over the fear of making a mistake and just get it done.

If a mistake is made, you can always come back and fix it later.

No matter what business you're in, you're going to be faced with starting new things on a regular basis. If you tend to get stuck, or have a hard time starting – try focusing on completion, not perfection.

Wisdom nugget:

Did you know that the movie-making industry thrives on this principle? For a multi-billion dollar profession, it's quite fascinating, actually.

There's a saying in Hollywood that goes: "It's not in the writing, it's in the rewriting." Especially when it comes to sitcoms or screenplays, apparently the first draft of something is expected to be really rough and 'barely hang together.'

Why? Because it's far easier to refine something that exists, than start from scratch. It's far easier to refine something into a masterpiece than try to write a masterpiece from the start.

Life isn't written in permanent ink, the last time we looked. It's flexible, with lots of room to grow and learn along the way. If you try on the attitude that 'it's all fixable,' you may find you can really let loose a bit more, stop agonizing over things, and enjoy the journey of business.

What is something you've been procrastinating about? Would it help you get started if you focus on completion, as opposed to perfection?

How can you benefit from focusing on completion, not perfection in your business?

CHAPTER 18
Seeking the Minimum Level

Would you use a power tool to put in a tack? Time and energy are your precious resources. Use them wisely by seeking the minimum level.

18

The idea of seeking the minimum level in business owes origins to the work of the Frugal Zealot, also known as author Amy Dacyczyn.[1] Amy first wrote about 'the minimum level' from the perspective of thrift as an alternative lifestyle in 1992.

'People are creatures of habit.'[2]

When it comes to business owners, there's never been a truer statement. That's why we figure the unexpected ways we talk about business are so well-received – they literally surprise you into opening your mind.

After hearing the same lessons about business for so long, we can tend to accept them without questioning. After doing things for the same way for so long, it can take a little shock treatment for us to stop.

But it's important that we do, because far too many business owners are chronically tired and overworked, yet are still trying harder to do more with their energy and time.

Old ways of thinking and old habits can be very costly – to both the success of your business, and your overall happiness.

CASE STUDY:

ANDREA

I was working with a client in the summer of 2002. I remember it clear as day. She was a really earnest, really serious-about-getting-to-success type of client. And she was talking about doing some door-to-door canvassing of the business owners in her building to see if there was interest in doing a building-wide flyer.

(This was part of our work together on collaboration – see Chapter 12: No Great Thing is Accomplished Alone)

Now you need to know that her business was doing alright. She had earned close to six-figures each year for the last year and a half and had an assistant and a nice little office. But whatever reason – you might relate – she was extremely stressed about getting over six figures. It was a prize for her, something symbolic, I think.

When she started talking about going from door-to-door herself, later in the day, and how it would take her several days to get around to all the offices,

> I interrupted.
>
> "I think that's a waste of your time and energy. You're already tired out as it is. Is this something YOU have to do?"
>
> I don't know why, but some clients just like to argue with their coach, and that's what she did. Finally, I said –
>
> "Why would you use a power tool to put in a tack?"
>
> And she got it.

Do you invest too much energy into tasks that aren't worth it? Are you using a lot of time on a project that could be done with much less?

If you have a tack in front of you, you wouldn't use a power tool to put it in, right? It would be a massive, disproportionately powerful tool to get the result you want.

This can be a difficult one, but try to develop an awareness of how to apply just the right amount of energy and resources to the appropriate tasks.

If you're used to providing a full-fledged proposal for a client, would a two-page summary work just as well? Do you send over five possible ideas for how to 'redo the living room' when 3 would be equally delightful to your client? How about paperwork – are you overdoing your paperwork and losing time and resources?

When you write emails, do you always proofread and double-check before you send out? If you're doing a series of follow-up calls that are administrative in nature, could an assistant could do the trick? Do you always stay open an extra three hours on Thursday night when only a few customers ever come in? See if closing up shop on Thursday nights will work. Or, take appointments for people who absolutely can't get to your store during regular hours.

You get the picture. Experiment with the minimum level.

Wisdom nugget:

Based on experience, we estimate business owners waste an average of 20-30% on tasks that would be just as good, just as complete, if they'd leave well enough alone.

The Frugal Zealot puts it really well:

> "When you wash dishes, do you always fill the sink to the top? If you're doing a small number of dishes a sink half full of water may suffice just as well. Do you always put a two-second squirt of dishwashing liquid in the water? See if a one-second squirt will work."

> "Do you use an inch of toothpaste because a brush has inch-long rows of bristles and every toothpaste

advertisement you've ever seen portrays a neat, full, bristle-length swath? Experiment to see if a ½ inch of toothpaste works as well."[3]

Seeking the minimum level definitely goes against the grain at first, because business owners are used to working hard, and racing to keep up.

Take a moment now to think of just one thing that you could work a lot less hard at to complete, or better yet, one thing you can take off your 'To Do' list entirely.

REVIEW AND RECAP: MEANING

Before you move on to the 'Beyond' section of the book, let's stop for a moment to refresh what's gone before.

We've now arrived at the end of the 'Meaning' section in this book about money, meaning and beyond. What's had the biggest impact on you so far, and how will it change how you go about your business?

11. **Are you making gravy without even knowing it?** One way to get more done in less time is make more use out of what you're already doing. How can you?

12. **No Great Thing is Accomplished Alone.** Being a martyr is highly unattractive. How can you give – and receive – more help?

13. **Picking the Ripe Apples** is a great habit to get into, especially if you're tired of forcing your way to success.

14. **Excuse Me, Will You Be My Google?** Are you overlooking this easy way to provide value to your clients? Be a filter…you're doing it anyway, you may as well take advantage!

15. **The Lone Ranger Syndrome** is a very common one. Even if you think you can't afford the help, you can – at least a little. Care to start now?

16. **Like whisking a dressing in a Salad Bowl**, you can lean on your physical (and other) environment. What's one thing you could improve today that would make a difference?

17. **Remember - the Clay is Never Dry.** Focus on completion, not perfection.

18. **Seeking the Minimum Level.** You wouldn't use a power tool to put in a tack, so don't send your 'big guns' out to do the little things in your business.

    Your energy will be the better for it.

Now, are you ready to go 'beyond' money and meaning in your business? Turn the page to get started.

BEYOND

*"People say that what we're all seeking is
a meaning for life.*

*I think we're really seeking an experience of being
alive… so that we can actually feel the rapture of life."*

Joseph Campbell

CHAPTER 19
Pulling a Costanza

When you're stuck, stop.
Turn yourself around and try doing the opposite.

19

You're probably familiar with a television sitcom called 'Seinfeld.'[1] Whether you've watched the show once or too many times, you probably remember that one of Jerry Seinfeld's friends was a character named George Costanza.

George was one of those people who couldn't do anything right. In his thirties, he still lived at home, had no job, no relationship and was losing the rest of his hair. Oh and yes, he was short and generally thought of as unattractive.

He put it something like this:

> *George:* It's not working, Jerry. It's just not working.
>
> *Jerry:* What's not working?
>
> *George:* Why did it all turn out like this for me? I had so much promise. I was personable, I was bright. Oh, maybe not academically speaking, but ... I was perceptive. I always know when someone's uncomfortable at a party. It became very clear to me sitting out there today, that every decision I've ever made, in my entire

> life, has been wrong. My life is the opposite of everything I want it to be. Every instinct I have, be it something to wear, something to eat ... it's all been wrong.

Sound familiar? We all have our 'George' days, when we feel like we're getting nowhere, and we don't know what to do about it. We feel miserable and unworthy, useless and helpless. We feel like George.

But one day, in one of the 'Seinfeld' episodes that takes place in their neighborhood diner, George has an epiphany. In all his frustration, he decides on a lark to do the 'opposite'.

> **Waitress:** Okay and how about you? What'll you have?
>
> **George:** The usual...tuna on toast...
>
> **Waitress:** Tuna on toast, coleslaw, cup of coffee.
>
> **George:** Yeah. No, no, no, wait a minute. I always have tuna on toast. Nothing's ever worked out for me with tuna on toast. I want the complete opposite of tuna on toast.
>
> Chicken salad on rye, un-toasted, with a side of potato salad and a cup of tea.
>
> **Elaine:** Well, there's no telling what can happen from this.

Chapter 19: Pulling a Costanza

At that moment, the camera shows a beautiful woman at the diner turning around and looking George right in the face from across the room. Eyes glowing, she says, "That's exactly what I ordered."

When you're stuck, spinning your wheels, or just generally feeling thwarted by life, stop pushing your energy in the same stuck direction.

Instead, try the opposite. Close your eyes for just one moment and visualize yourself turning around. Now, open your eyes.

You might be surprised at what looks you in the face.

CHAPTER 20
Where Are You Coming From?

Are people ignoring you and what your business has to say? Break through the sound barrier with examples from an enlightened Golf Course.

20

Where Are You Coming From and Why Does it Matter?

This elusive but important mindset shift was prompted by a question from one of our long-time readers:

> "Andrea, I appreciate your message. I am however, most impressed by your 'influencing language'. I'm wondering, what is your source of learning that skill? What can you pass on to us? Again, more than your message, your language and metaphor reaches the subconscious, inspires and engenders belief."

Here's Andrea's reply:

This is at once a truly fantastic question and a difficult one to answer. However, on a walk with my dogs one day, I saw some signs on the fence of a golf course that will help make the point. Read on to see for yourself.

The short answer to the question is "focus on your 'Come-From' rather than any 'technique' of writing."

Your ability to communicate well - persuasively and genuinely - will have an enormous impact on your business success, especially if you have written communications you use in promotions both on and offline.

In your efforts at building your business, do you spend time honing writing techniques, speaking skills or networking confidence?

A lot of people do.

And while this isn't wasted time per se, in my experience is that the better investment is in figuring out something called a 'come-from.' Yours, to be exact.

What exactly is a 'come-from?'

It's your mindset. The direction in which your thoughts go, your point of view, your worldview, your attitude, where you sit or stand, and even what direction you point your feet.

In general speech, do you say "but" a lot, when you could say "and?"

When chatting with a client or customer, do you say "you" versus "us?"

How often does your business say "no" to the outside world, whether that be to vendors, clients, or to internal team members?

Chapter 20: Where Are You Coming From?

Whether you know it or not, you have an internal bias that shows up as a 'place' that you come from, and this 'come-from' has a very strong impact on how you conduct your business. Not to mention how well your business is perceived, especially online.

More than anything, the power of your writing is driven, colored, and sometimes 'tainted' by your 'come-from'

To help with this, here is a concrete example of a come-from that shifted in a positive direction. (This is what I saw on my dog walk.) Now, the before and after effect is quite dramatic, so I have no doubt you'll understand it intellectually, but as an extra challenge, see if you can feel the difference in your body as well as your mind.

This particular dog walk is a lovely one that borders on the Bow River in the southeast side of Calgary. Part of it butts up against a driving range called Riverside Golf Park.[1] Probably two or three times each walk, my dogs and I find golf balls on the non-driving-range side of the very high fence.

Here is an old sign posted on the fence, for all of us dog walkers to see.

OLDEST OF 3 SIGNS

You can see how old it is because you can hardly read it, right? Not to worry, by looking at it closely in real life, I can tell you it says "ALL GOLF BALLS ARE THE PROPERTY OF" above Riverside Golf Park.

And then it reads "Found Balls MUST be returned immediately." And then the 'No Exceptions' you can see clearly for yourself.

Well I don't know about you but when I first saw this sign I asked myself, rather cynically, "Oh no! And if I don't, are you going to send the Golf Ball Police after me?" But I digress.

Chapter 20: Where Are You Coming From?

Here's an updated version of the sign, hung on the same fence, but obviously newer:

NEWER SIGN

This one is a little less 'angry' isn't it? It's a little less imperative, and no longer presented in that dreaded red ink. Seems reasonable enough I suppose.

But here comes the real shift. This is the newest sign that's been hung on the same fence:

NEWEST OF 3 SIGNS

Oh my goodness, now we have it.

Can you feel the difference? Can you articulate it?

For one thing, nowhere does 'Riverside Golf Park' figure on the sign. Why? They figured it out. It's not about them or what they call themselves. It's about incentivizing the dog walkers, enlisting them, engaging them in something that's in it for them.

Chapter 20: Where Are You Coming From?

Get it? It's actually pretty breathless.

Whoever came up with this new sign deserves a huge medal in my opinion, for shifting the driving range from a pretty medieval mindset to an energetically evolved 'come from.' It's all in the come-from.

Can you apply a shift in your 'come-from' and transfer that to your own business?

Writing great copy, delivering great service, and creating repeat customers who spread the word about you really does stem from something as nebulous as this.

So...ask yourself...what is your come-from?

Might it be scaring off customers? How could you evolve your come-from to model generosity, abundance, love, attractiveness and therefore...create more business for yourself?

The signs above tell the story. Read them again and integrate the shifts. This stuff goes deep. Then write down five ways you can shift your come-from to be aligned with the values you embrace most.

This will improve your business not only from a profits point of view, but also from a meaning point of view...your business will begin to represent who you are in a fundamental way that will continue to bring you joy.

Believe it. It's one of the keys I've seen unlock businesses time and time again. Then again I've also seen it be the downfall of several others who just couldn't 'get' this.

A few more examples of great 'come-froms'

At a Pet Store a sign says 'Leashed Dogs Welcome' (not, 'No Pets Allowed')

At Commerce Bank of New Jersey[2], an internal policy that says 'One Yes, Two No' (Meaning that any one bank member has the authority to say yes to a customer, but two to say no…)

The Swedish Furniture store IKEA, before opening its new flagship store in Calgary, put up a large sign saying 'We're HIRING' on a highly traffic road. And only in small letters were the words 'now open!' The emphasis being the benefit to the city in terms of new jobs, as opposed to the fact the store is opening.

At the bottom of articles published online, a blurb saying 'Duplication permitted with full attribution' (Not, 'Duplication prohibited.')

On the inside cover of an ebook or website 'This ebook is for your exclusive enjoyment.' (Not, 'Sharing or transferring this ebook is illegal and punishable by law.') Yikes!

I think you're starting to get the idea. Think about your come-from.

CHAPTER 21
Time For Some Hair of the Dog

Ever feel like a fraud in your biz? Or, just stuck in a rut - again? Whatever your business is, if you're embarrassed or shy about it, it's just not going to work long term. Time for some hair of the dog.

21

Question: I'm totally stuck. I thought my business was going well, but I can't seem to get anywhere these days. It's like spinning my wheels in mud and getting deeper and deeper into ick. Plus, I have no energy anymore. When people ask me what I do, I just can't seem to care enough to tell them. Please tell me what is up?

Whether you're just starting out or been around the block a dozen times, the feeling of 'I have no idea why but there is no energy around here' is a common one to business owners of all stripes.

First thing's first. Remember, everything is energy. And when you're stuck, experience tells us there's something wrong inside - not something you're doing - that is creating the block.

So here's where the idea of Hair of the Dog comes in.

The phrase Hair of the Dog originally comes from Medieval times when physicians of the time prescribed real hair from a dog to treat dog bites.

You know, someone would come into the surgery with a dog bite. And they would get a mouthful of tonic made from hair of the dog that actually bit them.

Now we don't know if that worked from a medical perspective, but the phrase in modern times has come to characterize something more familiar, at least to some.

When you – or someone you know - has indulged a little too much in alcohol the night before, the morning after can be a bit of a trial.

And the phrase, "You need some hair of the dog" has come to mean, "Ya might wanna have another drink, buddy, it'll take the edge off your headache this morning."

It's been a little while since either of us has tried this personally, but we seem to remember it works.

So what does all this have to do with your business? A lot, actually.

If you're stuck in any way, or even if you're not stuck but you want to amp up your flow of energy, ask yourself this:

"In what way could I be applying the things I sell, teach or stand for, to myself?"

"How could I - more thoroughly - be doing what it is I tell my clients they should be doing?"

The answers you come up with are...well...the things you must do to get unstuck.

MINI CASE STUDIES:

- If you're a massage therapist, how often are you yourself going to a therapist to reap the benefits of your trade? A grumbly massage therapist whose back hurts and forehead is wrinkled from low energy isn't someone most people would go back to...

- If you're a financial advisor, how are your finances? We're not saying you have to be a millionaire to be a terrific financial advisor, but you must actively be pursuing what you believe is important in the realm of finances. If you aren't, how can you do right by your clients?

- If you are a dentist, how are your own teeth?

- If you teach cold calling, how often are you picking up the phone?

- If you're a coach or consultant, are you walking your own talk?

'Nuff said.

It's pretty simple really...albeit maybe a bit unexpected. When you start to apply the Hair of the Dog Principle, count on your energy starting to flow again. It's like taking a little booster shot in exactly the right spot.

Wisdom nugget:

Make a list of why you think people should do business with you. Be thorough. Start with as many as you can write down, and come back a couple times as you think of more.

Example: They'll save money. Or time. Or they'll have a lot of fun. Or...

Chapter 21: Time For Some Hair of the Dog

Now make a list of ways YOU can live these things yourself.

CHAPTER 22
How Does Your Sex Life Affect Your Business?

Want more money? Sure, mom may blush, but if you really want to earn more, you gotta play more. After all, a full and ecstatic life is the only real reason to be in business.

22

Let's take a moment here and think about pleasure.

No really, let's.

Take a moment and think about what a perfect day in your life would look like.

Close your eyes a moment if you'd like.

How much detail can you conjure up? How many of your senses are involved? Can you feel a warm breeze? Smell a ripe mango? Taste that favorite seafood meal? Or maybe feel the touch of a loved one holding your hand while chuckling at something you said.

The fact of the matter is, when business owners run into a speed bump, the most common solution they come up with is 'Work Harder.'

Work harder, stay at the office longer, keep the computer on 'just in case' and plain old make like a tyrant and lash out hard at their business.

We call it the 'brute force' method, and it doesn't work.

If this seems familiar, let us put it plainly: you're overdue for a time out. Stop throwing your life at the business in hopes your sacrifice will create a miracle.

Instead, pursue pleasure awhile, in whatever shape or form that takes for you.

 Whether that pleasure for you is sex, or not, doesn't much matter. But one thing we know for sure is this – to the degree you can enjoy life to its fullest, is the degree to which you'll succeed.

The less you work, the more swift and sure your working hours will be.

The more you learn to enjoy your five senses, the more your business will grow.

For those of you who aren't yet blushing, ask yourself, how much pleasure can you stand? When you lose yourself in the joy of a perfect moment, how much energy are you awakening and how much of that will reflect back on your business?

After all, if you have no life outside of work to live, why should your business thrive to begin with?

Pursue pleasure. Your sex life has a direct impact on your business, whether you're ready to hear it or not.

CHAPTER 22
Riding the Tiger

Just about to make it big? But feeling stressed and unsure, maybe even scared witless about the future? Loosen up and ride the tiger.

23

As you hold your heart and mind open to making money and meaning in your business, you will undoubtedly come to some forks in the road.

Some business owners hit a ceiling in their business. They reach a certain level of success and despite best efforts are unable to move past this invisible barrier to growth. This seems to happen frequently at the quarter million dollar mark, so we've nicknamed it the 'Quarter Million Dollar Speed Bump.'

Other business owners step right into the flow, and go beyond what they thought was possible. Success arrives at their doorstep in full bloom and it creates a sensation like free falling – wonderful if you're calm, terrifying if you're not.

No matter which category you find yourself in, the most common response is to 'do this' or 'try that' to regain momentum or equilibrium. In our experience, the solution

– if we can call it that - has little to do with 'doing' and much more to do with 'being'.

Wisdom nugget:

Come to realize that your business is not yours; it's only on loan to you.

YOU are *not* in control.

Whether you have children or not, you've likely heard the saying, "Children are not ours, they're only on loan to us."

Somewhere along the path to seven figures, often comes the realization that the same thing applies to your business. It's a foundational piece of the journey.

Sooner or later, you, the CEO, Founder, President, Owner, or whatever title you hold, realize that you are not in control, and the business is in actuality *not* yours. It hits you between the eyes. And regardless of your spiritual beliefs or personal faith, let's see if this makes a kind of sense:

Your business is really only on loan to you to shepherd awhile.

Different business owners respond to this very differently, so pause a moment now to make a note...how does this idea strike you?

Does it seem true, and feel freeing? Or does it feel odd and uncertain? Maybe it feels like something else entirely.

Well, let's say a little more. What does this mean, your business is only 'on loan' to you? Case in point is the real-life story of a multimillion-dollar business called CoachVille[1], an online training and resource company founded by the late Thomas Leonard.[2]

CASE STUDY (PART 1):

While I was General Manager of CoachVille, Thomas once said to me, "Andrea, you're managing a multimillion dollar business for me now. I need for you to know I expect you to manage it, not control it."

As you know beyond a doubt, any business with substance on its way to significant financial success takes on a life of its own. This was definitely the case at CoachVille.

Thomas said, "CoachVille is like a giant tiger, with a tail that thrashes around as it runs back and forth. Riding on its back, you can't control it, you can only ride with it and stay loose. From time to time, you might be able to lean into it with one knee or the other.

But whatever you do, if you try to control it, it will

break your back."

Literally. Since Thomas' words of wisdom I've personally witnessed business owners' proverbial backs being broken, and I'm pretty sure you can think of a few examples too, if you consider it a moment. Control is not the answer.

To apply this key to your own situation, ask yourself, "In what way am I trying to force my business in a certain direction?"

"How can loosening my grip on it, and listening deeply to how it wants to grow, help me nurture my business in a vibrant and organic way?"

As the owner of a business that serves others; and as a business owner who's looking for more than money, we have no doubt that your business – at its best - is here to elevate the lives of others. Now, are you ready for your business to coach and inspire you in return?

CASE STUDY (PART 2):

When asked what Thomas' plan was, for CoachVille, or where he was headed, his answer was usually "Nowhere" or "Who knows?" But internally the way he described it was this:

"Andrea, we don't work from a blueprint here. We

> have no idea what CoachVille will be in 2 years, much less 10. We're smart enough not to throw a pile of bricks on the ground and call it a house, but all we do is lay one brick at a time while holding a big space for great things to unfold, however they unfold."
>
> In other words, we trust. And in trusting, fundamentally, did CoachVille grow as speedily and elegantly as it did.

So here's the essence behind how to continue riding the tiger to more money and meaning:

The more you stop letting your ego grow your business, a little or a lot, the more capacity, energy, drive and sustainability you will have access to.

Letting go of your business in this manner takes courage. Along the way, you'll discover that cultivating this courage and letting go of control is exactly the right (slightly uncomfortable) thing to do at the fork in the road.

Now here are some exercises for your use, as befits your circumstance, to tease out this topic for you. We invite you to answer as many or few as you like in writing, right now.

What do you think that only you can do? (Tasks, projects, other parts of your business.) How can you reframe this and let go of what seemed un-let-go-able until now?

What have you been saying no to, and what would happen if you said yes? Try saying yes instead, even if you don't know how it will unfold. Just try.

Any given business can only grow as big as the person who is running it. Where can you grow as a person so your business can expand too? What three things can you do to step out of your business' way?

CHAPTER 24
Care to 'BOP' Your Market in the Head?

If you're going to be in business, be in business all the way – be a leader in your market.

24

Having come to one of our most favorite concepts, may we ask you a question?

What is the boldest, most outrageous, most provocative statement you can make in your niche market?

What stand can you take, for what you believe is important, true, or desperately needed?

If you believe there are both an art and a science to building a successful business, this definitely falls into the art category, and we offer no apologies for it.

As an active member of society, you are doubtless aware that if someone wants to buy something, they have dozens of choices as to where to buy it.

Whether it's dry cleaning or strawberries, a pair of glasses or used books…consumers have a mind-boggling amount of choice. So why should they spend their money with you, and not the other business down the street?

Of course, there is no one 'right' answer to this question, but figuring out what you believe in, and taking a stand for it in your business is an excellent start.

When the world is filled with options, the best solution is to give people a compelling reason to do business with you.

The words 'Bold', 'Outrageous' and 'Provocative', together form the acronym 'BOP'. And so our question becomes: What is your BOP statement? What do you stand for in your market?

A great BOP statement is particularly well named because you know a strong position statement when it bops you in the head.

Put another way, it's a mind-stopping thing, or a splinter in your brain.

MINI CASE STUDIES:

- **Nike's BOP Statement is their tagline. Just do it.**

    What is so BOP about this? It stands for action, and stands against apathy or inaction or inertia. Go for it. Life is too short.

    Because this statement has been around for so

long, it's not as BOP-like as it used to be. But if you hearken back to when Nike first stood up for 'Just doing it,' you'll remember how mind grabbing a statement it was. And to an extent, still is.

- **Saturn's BOP Statement is their 'no-haggle' policy.**

What's bold and outrageous about this? In a niche full of flexibly priced vehicles, Saturn stands for their belief in their customers' right to always get the best price. And not have to stress over haggling for a new car.

They believe buying a new car can be enjoyable again.

- **Starbuck's BOP position is in the design, layout and beauty of their stores.**

Their position is that coffee is more than a drink. It's an experience, a personal, enjoyable, vivid and sensual moment that we ought to savor. And that it's worth paying 500% more for!

Wisdom nugget:

The trouble is, as business owners, we're not often asked what we stand for. And yet we have a great opportunity to do just that. As a matter of fact, most of us – as simple human beings - are not conditioned to ask what we believe in. We walk around in a chemical soup of information and when pressed, can't actually say what we think. Think about it.

So how about accepting our invitation to make your business meaningful at a different level? Cultivate a habit of nurturing clarity around what you stand for.

Ask, if you had just 60 seconds to say something to a person in your target market, what would it be?

If you had just 60 seconds to express what you'd like your life to stand for, what would that be?

CASE STUDY:

One of the wonderful things about traveling is having friends take you to their favorite restaurants. While in Denver last month, I had the pleasure of experiencing a meal at a tiny French Restaurant called Le Central.[1]

Excerpted here is their bold statement that without a doubt keeps them busy as one of the oldest standing restaurants in downtown Denver.

The Leisure Lunch

Take your afternoon back, bring your friends, bring your special someone.

To encourage the renewal of the leisure lunch, with each main course, Le Central will offer a $10.00 wine flight of five 3 ounce servings of wine...

AND...

All House Martinis at $2.00

AND...

All Desserts at $2.00

What can you - a business owner in pursuit of money, meaning and beyond - learn from this example?

If a restaurant can stand for something as important to them as the forgotten 'leisure lunch'...you can stand for something too.

What do you stand for? What do you believe? In what way are you willing to be a leader in your market and 'BOP' them in the head?

CHAPTER 25
The Sun and the Wind

Sick of trying so hard?
Are you being the sun or the wind?

25

Question: When you're trying to sell something to someone, I know it's important to communicate with people more than once. I've already emailed my newsletter readers with four different offers this month, but they still aren't buying. What should I write in my next email that will work? I'm tired of pounding them so many times."

With thanks to Aesop[1], let's paraphrase a little story. It may give you a new perspective on this as well as other situations where you feel like you're trying awfully hard.

The Sun and the Wind decided to have a little game. They agreed to prove which one of them was more powerful.

When a man came traveling down the road, they seized their opportunity – they decided to see who could make the man remove his coat, thus proving whether the Sun or the Wind was the more powerful.

The Wind took the challenge and began to blow. He blew as hard as he could at the man, trying to get him to remove his coat.

But the more the wind blew, the more the man clung to his coat and hat, and the wind had to give up.

Next the sun gave it a try and turned up his rays so it began to warm up. As the day grew brighter and the man grew warmer, he naturally found it too hot to keep his coat on and was happy to take it off.

Coming up on a small stream, he even took his shoes and socks off and took a wade before he continued on his journey.

With this story as a backdrop, let's get back to the above questions:

"How do I stop chasing after customers and get them to try (or buy) my stuff?"

"How do I stop trying so hard to get results?"

These are very common questions for business owners and the answers are in the parable on the previous page.

Ask yourself how you can be the sun, and not the wind.

How can you step into the river of your customer's natural desires, rather than chase after them waving your company brochure as they go down a different path?

Chapter 25: The Sun and the Wind

The saying goes, the only smart place to put a hot dog stand is in front of a crowd of hungry people.

Between the wind and the sun, which would you rather be, as you pursue the natural, effortless, stress-free growth of your business?

CHAPTER 26
The Paul Principal

Wondering if there's a true-blue 'secret' to business success? For better or worse, it's all about you.

26

Are you working as diligently, deeply and unflinchingly on *you* as you POSSIBLY can?

We don't mean your accounting, consulting, graphic design, veterinary, writing, speaking, lawn mowing, or other business-specific skills.

We don't mean your marketing skills.

We don't mean in (only) an analytical, examining kind of way.

We're talking about on you. The whole you. Who you are. What you stand for. How you behave. What you believe. If you have any hesitation about saying yes, here it is:

Time to do something about it.

Wisdom nugget:

You may be familiar with a concept in business circles that's often referred to as the 'Peter Principle.'

The Peter Principle is a theory originated by Dr. Laurence Peter in his book by the same name.[1] In simple terms, the principle says that in any given business, an employee will tend to rise to his level of incompetence.

Or, basically, they'll keep getting promoted until they're terrible at their new position, like the factory worker whose terrific performance gets him promoted to a management role, which he fails at.

Well, there's a new principle we'd like to introduce you to, which we call the Paul Principle. It says:

In any given business, the growth of the business will rise or fall to the level of the business owner's personal development.

We see this frequently. When people grow, their business grows. When people don't, their businesses don't. And sometimes, when businesses get inherited or acquired, the business will show a spurt or dive, based on the ethos of the new owner.

CASE STUDY:

At an internet marketing seminar some time ago, I saw an example of the Paul Principle at work in the starkest of ways.

At the request of the coach speaking at the front of the room, a young man about 20 walked to the front of the room. There, he was asked "What's your big dream?" To which he replied, "To start a record label so great bands can get the attention they deserve." (Pretty articulate, considering.)

"Okay, that's great," said the coach. "So what's stopping you, why aren't you going for it?"

And the young man – we'll call him Jay - said, "I don't have the money I need to do it."

"Fair enough." And the coach turned away to face the audience. "So based on what you've heard, is there anyone in the audience who would like to invest some money into making Jay's dream of a record label come true?"

Hands shot into the air, including mine. Actual dollar bills, ten dollar bills and more were waved around.

> The coach turned to Jay at this point and said, "Jay, you have 3 minutes, starting now, to tell these good people why they should give you their money." And he started the timer on his watch.
>
> What do you think happened next?
>
> The time, simply and quietly, slipped by with Jay saying not a single word, and the coach's "Time's Up" was met with hushed tones.
>
> And Jay walked back – miserable certainly, and shocked, for sure – to the protection of his seat among his friends.

Putting aside the question of this style of coaching – this true story illustrates a potent thing.

When opportunity knocks, are you ready?

If you knew you could have everything you wanted right now, would you know what to say?

Are you – your character, your development, your greater Self – ready?

If there is one thing we invite you to really embrace as you go about life in the next thirty days, it's this. Work the Paul Principle. Make it work for you by:

- Saying NO to bland. Stand for something.

- Cultivating a vision. Get clear about what you believe and mean it. Lead.

- Conditioning yourself emotionally. You and your business will weather many ups and downs. Nurture your strength of spirit just like you work out your body for the great race.

- Articulate what you want and why. Don't worry about how just yet.

- Being prepared to say a resounding 'yes' to help that wants to find you, and that many times, is sitting right on your doorstep.

Be diligent and unflinching about yourself and your growth. Start now in whatever shape or form that looks like to you.

Your success (financial and other) as a business owner is DIRECTLY linked to your ability to evolve yourself. It's the Paul Principle and it's at work in each and every one of us. Remember it.

Wisdom nugget:

One of the ways to work on yourself is to take stock of where your life is now.

Consider taking just 30 minutes now to take the simple and insightful self-test called the 'Clean-Sweep Assessment' and score your life out of 100 points.[2]

CHAPTER 27
Re-learning How to Swim

Been doing things the same way for forever? Just like this story about swimming, could it be time to destroy old habits and create some new?

27

A story from Tina...

I had the best darn swim of my life recently.

After doing my first triathlon I decided that I wanted to improve my swimming. Surfing the 'net one day I came across the Total Immersion (TI) website.[1]

There are a few free videos on the site that show the TI method of swimming. I was instantly drawn by the beauty and grace of this style of swimming - it's like nothing I've seen before. So I bought the book to learn more.

Total Immersion swimming is about creating a more efficient stroke in the water, so that each lap is enjoyable and sustainable. They call this 'fishlike' or 'slippery' swimming, with the intent being to slip your body through the smallest possible hole in the water. The human body is not built to swim, and this style of swimming is as close to the movement of a fish as the human body can get.

Most people (myself included) are taught to swim by using brute force - arms pumping and legs kicking as hard as possible to move through the water. Not only is this tiring, it is tough to improve your swimming results over time as your arms and legs can only go so fast.

Following the advice of the TI book, I decided to stop my inefficient swimming style right then and there and follow the TI drills to learn a new way of swimming. So for 4+ weeks I started doing the drills, working my way through the complete series of drills as instructed in the book.

At the end of one of my drill practices I decided to try and swim a lap, just for fun. Let me tell you, I was pleasantly surprised. It was the best lap of swimming I had ever done! I felt like a totally new person in the pool... my breathing was effortless, I felt a natural flow and rhythm in my stroke.

AND I shaved off a whole 6 strokes per lap from my old style of swimming. 6 strokes! That's a 25% improvement. Now I'm no swimming pro, but from what I understand of swimming in general and my own experience to date that is A HUGE improvement to make in just over a month.

It was the coolest darn thing. I learned how to swim in a totally different way - a much easier and enjoyable way. So much so that I couldn't wait to get in the pool again, and I had a silly grin on my face the rest of the day.

It got me wondering, what else in my life could I look to 're-learn'?

Where else do I *struggle* to get the results I want? Where I'm tired and sometimes plain discouraged, working harder and harder with no end or real improvement in sight?

Taking a look at my business, I could definitely see some room for improvement there, especially in the areas that are 'stuck' and not working the way I would like.

Haven't you heard the saying regarding the definition of insanity? Something like, "The definition of insanity is doing the same things over and over again and expecting a different result."

When we get stuck in our businesses, it's quite often the result of doing the same things and expecting a different result. Even with a massive outpouring of energy and time, if something is no longer working then there is no way around it – it's no longer working.

How to fix this?

The simple answer is to do something different. We know, that seems quite obvious, but this can actually be quite difficult. In order to do something new, it usually requires that we first stop doing the 'old' things. And as creatures of habit this can be a huge challenge for many of us. It is easier to hang onto the same old way of doing things, even when it no longer works.

We sometimes like to call this 'creative destructionism' in business. In order to create something new you must first destroy the old. In order to take ten steps forward you must first take a step backwards. Like Tina's swimming improvement, this is big stuff, and definitely requires courage, fortitude and conviction to try in business.

CASE STUDY:

> Thomas Leonard, founder of CoachVille, the largest coach training and membership organization in the world, was also a big proponent of destroying something in order to create something new.
>
> The best example of this was when he decided to take a $79 membership and make it free. In doing so, he closed down a five-figure revenue stream – an act of courage for any business owner. The result? Membership spiked from 12,000 to close to 25,000 in just a few months.

Nature does the same thing doesn't it? Tornados, forest fires, and even earthquakes, although causes of great devastation, also create something vigorous and new in their wake, given time.

Could it be that it's time to creatively destroy something in order to make room for something bigger and better?

Where is your business currently stuck?

What is no longer working for you, even if it used to work quite well?

A FINAL RECAP: BEYOND

All good things must come to an end, and that includes this book! Before moving on, let's do a final recap.

A Final Recap

The chapters in the 'Beyond' section are particularly powerful when integrated over time. Put a star next to the ones that speak to you the most:

19. **Pulling a Costanza** may seem counter-intuitive, but the rewards can be worth it. When in doubt, try doing the opposite.

20. **Where Are You Coming From?** Very often it's not what you say it's how you say it. Will you let the three golf course signs be a reminder of this to you?

21. **Perhaps it's Time for Some Hair of the Dog.** Walking your talk – or not – will impact your bottom line dramatically. So are you?

22. **Your Sex Life Affects Your Business!** Talking about your sex life isn't just a gimmick. Great sex – and other great pleasures in life – will benefit your business, period.

23. **What Do You Stand For, In Your Market?** Rather than just running a great business, we invite you to be a leader in your market. How about it?

24. **The Sun and the Wind** epitomize two types of business people. Which are you?

25. **Are you ready to ride the tiger of your business?** Remember to stay loose.

26. **The Paul Principle is all about you.** Are you ready for what you say you want?

27. **Could you benefit from Re-learning How to Swim?** Don't be afraid to slip backwards a little to make big progress.

And now, it's time to wrap things up. Read on for practical next steps and additional resources.

Practically Speaking, What's Next?

For those of you who tend towards the pragmatic or linear way of thinking, congratulations for sticking your way through this book! And even if you're not one of those, you may be asking...what next? What should I do?

How can you start to apply the business principles in this book, from a strictly practical point of view?

Well, we'd like to share a secret with you. It's the one thing that you should *always* keep in mind - what we affectionately call the Caramilk Secret of building your business.

Remember those Caramilk commercials from the 1980s? The ones that made the secret of the Caramilk chocolate bar seem like such rocket science, when in reality all they're doing is making a chocolate bar - it can't be that tough!

Business can be much the same. On the surface it can seem complex, and many business books and programs would have you believe it is. But in reality there is one clear step to begin putting the principles in this book into practice. It's simple and easy and once you do it, you can build a strong foundation for your ongoing business growth.

Get permission to be in touch with people in your market by collecting their email address.

Create a Pink Spoon based on the concepts in Chapter 1, put it on a one-banana website based on the concepts in Chapter 6; and from there you can start to apply everything else. 'The Paul Principle', the 'Fastest Path to Money', all of the Chapters in the book, in fact.

But it all begins with being able to make real connections with real people and an email address remains the simplest most efficient way to do that sustainably.

Regardless of what business you are in, this is your *real* job… to focus on building and nurturing relationships for as long as your business exists.

And do so in a way that's meaningful and sustainable in the long run, to you.

In Conclusion

And so we come to the end of this book.

Before signing off, we'd like to emphasize just three final things we feel most strongly about.

First, everything – no exceptions – is energy.

Our biggest hope for you is that this book has given you an inner calm and invigorated sense of energy for your business and your life. The 27 everyday unexpected things in these pages are just another way of affirming for you that all the wisdom you need to succeed is right within reach.

It all pivots on how you look at things.

As you experiment with the vast stores of creative 'juice' in each chapter, begin to cultivate a habit of harnessing that energy in your work.

Running your business does not have to be hard, or boring, or theoretical. Or dry and technical. There are no 'shoulds.' You get to choose. Everything around you has something to teach if you'll only listen.

So if this book has given you energy, please use it as a tool; when you'd like a boost, pick it up, read a few pages and see what happens.

Just try not to do it before bedtime! (Or you may not get any sleep...)

Second, how you do anything is how you do everything.

What will you do as a result of connecting with the paradigm shifts in this book? How thoroughly will you begin to live them?

A great way to begin to integrate new concepts is to discuss and debate them, and hold yourself accountable to trying them in real life, not just in your head.

So we invite you to do just that. Pick one of the concepts – perhaps it's the 'Paul Principle' – and discuss it with a colleague or business partner. How would the 'Paul Principle' idea land with them, do you think?

Or how about 'Pulling a Costanza?' Could one of your frustrated suppliers get a kick – and a light bulb moment

– from you sharing this gem from the TV show Seinfeld, of all places?

Better yet, share the idea of the 'Sun and the Wind' with a child in your life – yours or not. You might be surprised how it changes the way they run their lemonade stand come summer time.

In short, try living some of your favorite 'unexpected ways to create what really matters.'

Finally, we don't do anything by halves.

By this point in the book it's probably quite clear to you – we have a secret agenda.

For us, life and business are inseparable. Sure our businesses provide us with a terrific livelihood. But they also give us the opportunity to pursue a meaningful life of our choosing. There is no dividing line.

By titling the book the way we have - 'Money, Meaning & Beyond' – and writing the book the way we have using out-of-the-box concepts and side doors - we hope we've helped transform the way you relate to your business in this bigger-picture way.

Because in the final analysis, it's about more than money, isn't it? You truly can have it all.

Even without knowing you personally yet, we take our hats off to you for your decision to do great things every day.

We hope you'll continue to build and grow yourself and your business with your head, your heart and your spirit.

> "One does not see well but with the heart. The essential is invisible to the eye."
>
> -'The Little Prince' by Antoine de Saint-Exupery

Do stay in touch. We'd love to hear from you as your life unfolds.

And finally, thank you for the privilege of sharing these thoughts and walking the talk with you. It truly is an honor.

Best wishes!

Additional Tools, Resources and Invitations

Getting 'virtual assistance' for your business may be on your radar this minute, or it may not appear for months.

When the time is ripe, the Multiple Streams 'Dream Team' of Virtual Assistants is at the ready, excited by the prospect of helping you make money and meaning in your business.

> "Our newest VA is working out **WONDERFULLY!!!**
>
> *Since she arrived, we've all gotten 100% more organized (which is saying a lot), she's lightened the burden of my original VA significantly, and she's a true problem solver, adding new systems and procedures that really work. AND she's great fun to work with!*
>
> *A priceless addition to our team – we all appreciate her energy and insights, and I think together we're going to be able to reach our goals for 2006!*
>
> *The 'Dream Team' are THE professionals I turn to when I need to find new virtual assistance."*
>
> - Suzanne Falter-Barns
> www.GetKnownNow.com

If you're ready to investigate how you can increase income and pursue the meaningful life you desire with the help of a Virtual Assistant, be sure to request a copy of the special report, "101 Things a VA Can Do For You."

The report, and more information about finding a VA is available by visiting the Dream Team's home on the web at www.MultipleStreamsTeam.com.

....

After reading and absorbing 'Money, Meaning & Beyond' you may find yourself interested in pursuing the 'Beyond' part of the equation more deeply.

A good way to find out if this is you is by reading this quote:

> The world is awash in money! Do you hear what that means? It is awash in money. It is flowing for everyone. It is like Niagara Falls. And most of you are showing up with your teaspoons.
>
> *- Abraham-Hicks*

If you find yourself moved to explore this idea, we invite you to discover a fun and empowering way to activate your ability to create prosperity – from the inside-out.

Additional Tools, Resources and Invites

The Prosperity Game, first introduced by Abraham-Hicks (teachers of Deliberate Creation) is available to everyone to play, by visiting the website below.

> *"The most powerful course on prosperity I know, because it truly brings the concepts into our being on a much deeper, more permanent level..."*
>
> - Namaste, Kathleen C.

Visit www.ChoosingProsperity.com to begin playing the Prosperity Game.

> *"If, now, there is something you choose to experience in your life, do not 'want' it -- choose it.*
>
> *Do you choose success in worldly terms? Do you choose more money? Good. Then choose it. Really. Fully. Not half-heartedly."*
>
> - Conversations with God, Book 1

....

Part of being a leader in your market is stepping up and getting known for what you believe is true. Perhaps thinking big about this has inspired you? Why not go all the way and:

- Publish your own book.
- Be featured on television, or get your own show!

- Be frequently quoted in magazines or on popular websites.
- Become nationally and internationally recognized as an expert in your field.

Luckily, getting known is something that is easily done if you know the right steps, and the right people.

If you knew you could naturally attract the media in a way that is uniquely you – and it would bring you a much larger potential client base – would you pursue it?

> *"After I pitched my book to an Executive Editor, he told me he wished all authors understood publishing the way I did. You helped me break in!"*
>
> *- Persephone Zill*

Visit www.TimeToGetKnownNow.com for more info about the 'Get Known Now' Multimedia Home Study Program. Readers of 'Money, Meaning & Beyond' will receive $50 off the price of the program at this website only.

> *"**Get Known Now** has absolutely stunned me, with its wealth of information, resources, and step-by-step guidance in some of the toughest aspects of promotion and marketing. In only two days since I first downloaded the book, I have applied several new techniques from the book, and they are already yielding stellar result..."*
>
> *- Marney Makridakis*

More resources from the authors of **Money, Meaning & Beyond: 27 Unexpected Ways to Create What *Really* Matters for Business Owners:**

- **Are you ready to create your own Pink Spoon? So are many other business owners just like you!**

    Join the Pink Spoon Community and brainstorm, get peer feedback and moral support to launch your own Pink Spoon. While you're there, help others along their way as well!

    Go to **www.MoneyMeaningandBeyond.com** to get started.

- **Would you like to experience a real-life example of a Pink Spoon, written by Tina and Andrea?**

    Visit **www.PinkSpoonMarketing.com** and input your email into the blue box part way down.

- **Would you like to participate on monthly open TeleSeminars to discuss the concepts in the book, 'Money, Meaning & Beyond?'**

    Visit **www.MakeMoneyandMeaning.com** to reserve your seat and get ready to participate!

> "The call "What the Heck is Pink Spoon Marketing™" was a helpful way for me to further synthesize these concepts. These resources are supporting me in taking my next steps into doing the work more fully that I feel called to do. Much thanks for easing me into greater focus, increased clarity, and real action."
>
> - Diana

....

After reading Chapter 4: The Fastest Path to Money - are you keen to find yours?

Often the fastest path to money is right under your nose; it just takes an experienced guide to help you shine a light on it.

If you think a 1-on-1 mentoring environment focused on you and you business would be of help, the Multiple Streams Coaching Team would be delighted to hear from you.

> "Tina jam packs her coaching sessions with so much no-nonsense, solid information it's almost overwhelmingly inspiring. After talking to her, I have a clear action plan to follow, and I'm totally confident I can accomplish my online marketing goals!"
>
> - Stacey Morris, Service Business Coaching

Coaching Packages available for 1-on-1 attention by an experienced Multiple Streams Coach.

- One Lightning Round Session (60 mins).
- Three 45-minute Calls per month.
- Or Save 10% by committing to 90 Days of coaching in advance*.

   *With 90 Days of Coaching in Advance you receive a complimentary copy of Pink Spoon MarketingTM: The Art & Science of Building a Multiple Streams Business, a 189-Page Workbook and 5 Audio CDs (retail: $497).

Due to the intense nature of the relationship, 1-on-1 coaching spaces are limited. Visit **www.MultipleStreamsCoaching.com** to inquire.

....

> *"I've used just a smidge of 'Pink Spoon Marketing*^{TM}*' and my business has exploded!*
>
> Andrea and Tina pull back the curtain behind what really works for today's successful businesses with a complete, comprehensive blueprint for success. Clueless? Get this book! Think you're not clueless? You still need to get this book!"
>
>   - Andy Wibbels, Creator, Easy Bake Weblogs Seminar, Podcasting Bootcamp, RSS Essentials, BizSlap, **www.GoBlogWild.com** and Author of BlogWild!

Save $100 on Pink Spoon Marketing – a step-by-step Multimedia Home Study Program to help you launch your Pink Spoon, and fill your Multiple Streams funnel with products and services that bring your business more money, your way.

Pink Spoon Marketing™ is your personal 'coach in a workbook' without the monthly fees. Especially suited for self-starters and do-it-yourselfers!

Offer only available to readers of 'Money, Meaning & Beyond' for a limited time.

Visit www.PinkSpoonMarketing.com/Special to activate your $100 discount.

Endnotes

Introduction

1. The story about the five frogs was first published at the Team Me Teamwork Blog authored by Inventor Tom Heck. Tom introduces the idea that 'Deciding is not Doing' in his article "6 Key Principles For Facilitating A Team During a Period of Change." Publication date March 7, 2006. View other teamwork articles including this one by browsing www.TomHeck.Blogs.com.

Chapter 1:

1. "You can't solve a problem with the same mind that created it" is a quotation attributed to Albert Einstein. More commentary on this and Einstein's body of work is available online at the Einstein Archives Online at www.AlbertEinstein.info.

2. Worthwhile Magazine is a magazine dedicated to "Work with Purpose, Passion and Profit." Although it is a print magazine you can subscribe to, there is also a great online community that provides resources

and tools on the subject of worthwhile work (and the worthwhile lives that are the result.) If you're pursuing meaning with your money, you may find the website of interest – we certainly do. Find the site at www.WorthwhileMag.com,

3. A blog (or weblog) is a type of website in which messages are posted in a user-friendly way without the services of a web designer. When visiting a blog, it can look a lot like an online diary, as usually the newest content is at the top.

To learn more about blogs, we recommend the book GoBlogWild! by Andy Wibbels. For more resources and information about how to use a blog in a way that supports your business growth – and enjoy it along the way – visit www.AndyWibbels.com. You do not – repeat, do not – have to be terribly technically savvy to make a blog work.

4. Podcasting is like online radio. As a user of a podcast, you can download the audio clips directly to your computer and listen, or you can subscribe to a service that allows you to be notified when new audio is available. Podcasting utilizes a technology called RSS which some say is beginning to replace email in terms of efficiency and effectiveness when it comes to reaching people on the internet.

Chapter 2:

1. The idea that there are only three principal ways to increase income in your business is classic Jay Abraham. Jay is often referred to as America's Number One Marketing Wizard and is author of multiple best-selling titles including "Getting Everything You Can Out of All You've Got." Visit www.Abraham.com for more information about Jay and his line of books and CDs.

2. Wendy's website at www.WendyWeiss.com is an excellent model of what's possible when you tap into the desire lines of a specific group of people. Ask yourself if you can identify your clients as a group of people with a set of common problems or goals, and – important – you know how to reach those people. This may be through associations, online discussion groups, or perhaps in networking groups through your chamber of commerce.

   If you can do these two things, you will be able to tap into a rich vein of desire. Your business strategy becomes very simple. Provide the solutions to the problems being expressed by the desire lines in front of you, and get in front of them through their naturally occurring groups. People interested in selling naturally cluster together in various groups and have the same issues with making more sales. Have a closer look at Wendy's website at www.QueenofColdCalling.com, especially her products on the topic of Cold-Calling and 'Getting Past the Palace Guard.'

3. Desire lines can change over time. What was once a "hot thing" that a lot of people were seeking, may no longer be so "hot" after several years.

   Jennifer Louden's work on Comfort is a great example of taking advantage of a desire in the marketplace that did not previously exist. The concept of comfort the way Jennifer presents it is very modern, and is languaged that way as a result. To learn more about Jennifer Louden, also known as "The Comfort Queen," visit her online at www.ComfortQueen.com.

Chapter 4:

1. For more of Guy Kawasaki's wisdom, visit www.GuyKawasaki.com.

2. For more statements about why people do what they do, visit www.MoneyMeaningandBeyond.com/compelling/

3. Tom's website again is www.TeachMeTeamwork.com.

Chapter 5:

1. The concept of 'permission-based' marketing was given prominence by author Seth Godin, in his book called "Permission Marketing."

2. Collecting email addresses or mailing addresses can be automated using various tools. For email addresses specifically we use and recommend a system called Aweber. To find out more about the pros and cons of Aweber and some success stories of websites that use it, visit www.MoneyMeaningandBeyond.com/aweber/

3. The International Living website is a veritable treasure trove of information on how to live overseas. It's not only informative on this topic, it's also a great example of how an online business can be run in a meaningful and sustainable way. Visit them at www.InternationalLiving.com

4. TotalImmersion.net is also the subject of the final chapter in this book. To read more about how this site positively affected Tina's swimming and shone a light on a valuable business principle, see Chapter 27 entitled "Re-learning How to Swim."

Chapter 6:

1. Contrary to what you might think, many websites are not designed to maximize the chances of them making money, at least not directly. Often, you'll find that websites are created to enhance the reputation of the company, or simply act as an online 'brochure.'

Some websites though, are created with just the one goal – to make money. These are referred to as direct response websites and are the kind of website we recommend small businesses create. Because it doesn't matter how good-looking your website is if you don't make money from it and have to close down your business as a result.

Our affirmation on your behalf: "My website can directly earn me money and that is the kind of website I want." Remember this when you start talking to web designers.

2. The reference to 'one-Banana' comes from another book by author Seth Godin, this time 'The Big Red Fez.' Seth has a way of writing and teaching marketing that we enjoy and learn from regularly. If the 'one-Banana' concept of web design intrigues you, we highly recommend you read 'The Big Red Fez." It's a quick, easy and particularly appealing to business owners who want to be empowered to create real results with their websites, as opposed to the ones that just looking pretty.

3. To have a more detailed look at this website, visit it live on the Internet at www.FireYourWeddingPlanner.com.

4. What is a virtual assistant, or VA for short? Someone who can help do things for you in your business AND who isn't necessarily in your physical location. Virtual assistants are discussed in more depth in Chapter 15: The Lone Ranger Syndrome. When you are ready to pursue finding a virtual assistant to whom you can delegate your unfinished tasks, visit www.MultipleStreamsTeam.com for a recommendation to an affordable and skilled VA.

Chapter 7:

1. Solo-E.com is a is a lifestyle-inspired online learning and connection community dedicated to the success of Solo Entrepreneurs worldwide. To find out more, visit www.Solo-E.com.

2. For more information about how to lead no-fee Teleseminars so that they generate income, consider investing in something called "The Minute-By-Minute Template: How to Lead a Free TeleSeminar so You Make Money" available at www.MoneyMeaningandBeyond.com/tele-template/. The Minute-byMinute Template is a test-drive templated system that is proven to bring business in the door from free teleseminars.

Chapter 8:

1. John is web guru for Jillian Middleton, Head Coach of Savvy Sponsoring.com. Chapter 9:

1. For more details about how to measure what matters in you business, be sure to have a look at a sample metrics template available at www.MoneyMeaningandBeyond.com/metricstemplate

Chapter 11:

1. The Beanstalk Boys is part of the Supported Entrepreneurship Program (SEP) run by Calgary Alternative Support Services, a not-for-profit agency supported by

the Government of Alberta. Supported Entrepreneurship is a process that helps persons with disabilities develop and operate a small business, and in doing so expand their experience of life. Small business coaches are part of the process of making this happen.

If you're curious about the Beanstalk Boys and how they're doing, visit their website at www.BeanStalkBoys.com to see where their next seedling or vegetable sale is being held in the city of Calgary.

2. Book title: Signs of Hope, Working Towards our Common Future Oxford University Press, USA (July 1, 1990)

Chapter 12:

1. This parable was quoted in 'Ben & Jerry's Double Dip: How to Run a Values Led Business and Make Money Too' by Ben Cohen, Jerry Greenfield. Chapter 9: The Future of Values-Led Business, page 257. Simon and Schuster. 1998.

2. Archived issues of the Joy to the Planet project, including "How to Throw a Party and help the planet," "How to Earn a Living and help the planet" are available at www.JoytothePlanet.com.

3. The organization called Circle of Life is, at the time of printing, on sabbatical in preparation for the production of Julia Butterfly-Hill's book "Legacy of Luna" as

a major motion picture. You can however, still find out more and browse their archives at www.CircleofLife.org.

Chapter 13:

1. The concept of the ripe apples first came up during individual coaching sessions in winter 2005, and I (Andrea) use it regularly when working with clients on the issue of 'struggle.' During the writing of this book, I've been reading a novel by Gail Anderson-Dargatz called "The Cure for Death by Lightning" which contains a section that beautifully evokes the sensibility and intended message in 'Picking the Ripe Apples' - in much more vivid language. This segment takes the metaphor of ripeness in business to a different very sensual plane. From page 158 in the novel:

"If a raspberry is ripe, caressing it with your fingertips will bring the berry rolling into your hand. But wait for that ripeness. A berry plucked too early has no sweetness, only a coarse flavor that will pucker your lips up tight. When a berry is ready you'll know by its softness, the deep purple-red color, and the ease with which it gives itself to you."

Chapter 14:

1. Google is the world's best-known online search engine. If you haven't used it before, you can try searching for any piece of information – no matter how remote - at

www.Google.com. According to Google's own statistics, it processes more than 200 million requests for information per day in more than 80 languages.

The value of Google is of course, that it allows us to access the right pieces of information at the right time, and nearly instantly. In doing so, it makes sense of the Internet. In fact, it has been argued that without Google, the Internet would be useless, much like an encyclopedia would be useless if it were not organized alphabetically.

2. The idea of Google being a little like God has been debated widely on the Internet, however the original expression is attributed to Thomas Friedman in his book 'The World is Flat' where he states "Google is like God. God is wireless. God is everywhere. And God sees everything."

Chapter 15:

1. Often, business owners will procrastinate the task of hiring help, on the basis that they can't yet afford it. However just one simple question can help you see that there is, in fact, a point at which you cannot NOT afford it. If you are the only person in your business who can bring in income – by networking, designing a promotion, forming a partnership or otherwise – how much business is being lost when you choose to do administrative tasks?

Put it another way, if you pay $20 or $30 an hour to get a few hours of help each week, and in the empty time in your calendar, you focus intently on bringing in business to the tune of $100 an hour, that's clearly a good deal.

So ask yourself if you should stop procrastinating finding help. It's a mindset shift that all business owners must face if they want to be around for the long term. You do want that, right? We recommend you make the shift sooner rather than later.

2. As mentioned elsewhere, visit www.MultipleStreamsTeam.com if you are interested in taking a first step towards hiring a Virtual Assistant. If you're not sure you're ready yet, begin marinating in the possibilities by picking up a copy of the report "How a Virtual Assistant can help you increase your profits."

3. Jillian Middleton heads up a coaching business that specializes in helping network marketers succeed. Her no-nonsense, 'tell-it-like-it-is' approach has empowered her growing roster of clients at www.SavvySponsoring.com. We continue to be tickled and privileged by the opportunity to work intensively with Jillian as she 'BOP's this niche in the head.

4. Part of the solution to Jillian's fax challenge was to implement a portable fax service called www.eFax.com. If you're looking for a mobile fax solution that allows your assistant to organize faxes on your behalf, this could be your ticket.

Chapter 16:

1. Each year, many thousands of business owners turn to a business or life coach to help get their 'environment' set up in a way that supports them.

   Top-notch coaching on environments can declutter your life, accelerate your business growth, and give you renewed energy. Visit www.MultipleStreamsCoaching.com to explore coaching possibilities with a Multiple Streams Associate Coach, or to get a referral to a coach that best suits your needs at this time.

   For general information about coaching and coaches, visit Andrea's Blog at www.AndreaJLee.com/blog.

Chapter 17:

1. Bonita Joy Yoder, author of "Invest Like a Millionaire, and Sleep Like an Angel" was the first person to share this quote with us. To us, it was immediately evident that what applies to real estate applies to all businesses! Bonita takes a very different, spiritual approach to real estate investing which we find refreshing in a field

that's classically filled with the message "money, money, money." To find out more about how you can tap into your spiritual energy to inform your real estate investment, visit www.BonitaYoder.com.

2. Abraham-Hicks is a group of spiritual teachers on the topic of deliberate creation. Their words of wisdom are available via books, tapes and online excerpts. The latter are available at no charge at their website: www.Abraham-Quotes.com. Their main website is www.Abraham-Hicks.com.

Chapter 18:

1. The Frugal Zealot is the pen name for author Amy Dacyczyn, who founded the newsletter "The Tightwad Gazette" in 1990 and within two years saw subscriptions climb to over 100,000. Her newsletters have since gained even greater popularity in book form. You can find multiple volumes of this fun and enlightening read under the title "The Tightwad Gazette: Promoting Thrift as a Viable Alternative Lifestyle." Villard Books, 1993.

2. Amy's article "Seeking the Minimum Level" in volume one of her book was the inspiration for this chapter, which takes the idea of the minimum level and applies it to the business world. 'People are creatures of habit' is how Amy begins her article on page 85.

3. "The Tightwad Gazette" by Amy Dacyczyn, page 86.

Chapter 19:

1. Excerpted from the "Seinfeld" post at Wikipedia.org, "Seinfeld" was an American television sitcom set in New York City that ran from July 5, 1989, to May 14, 1998. It was one of the most popular and influential TV programs of the 1990s. In 2002, TV Guide released a list of the top 50 greatest shows of all time and ranked Seinfeld #1. To view sample video clips or episode outlines of Seinfeld, visit www.Seinfeld.com. You may be surprised to discover a slew of meaningful business lessons in each episode.

Chapter 20:

1. If you're ever in Calgary and want to see the three Golf Ball signs in person, go to the off-leash dog park located at the intersection of Southland Drive and Deerfoot Trail in South East Calgary. Once there, turn right towards the tall fenced area you'll see at the south end of the park. The three signs hang facing the river on the section of fence just past the pond.

2. Management 'UberGuru' and author of 'Re-Imagine!' Tom Peters first highlighted this customer service policy of the Commerce Bank of New Jersey (http://bank.commerceonline.com) at his blog. To find the specific post, go to http://www.tompeters.com/entries.

php?note=006710.php. To read more of Tom's wisdom, visit his home page at www.TomPeters.com.

Chapter 23:

1. CoachVille is an online global coaching community founded by Thomas Leonard in 2000. Andrea and Tina were General Manager and Assistant General Manager of CoachVille from 2001 to 2003. During that time, we were privileged to help it grow into a seven-figure enterprise with more than 39,000 members worldwide.

2. Thomas Leonard is often referred to as the founder of the professional coaching profession, and is author of "The Portable Coach" - the first book to comprehensively cover the principles of attraction. He died suddenly at age 47 in 2003. To read more about Thomas visit www.ThomasLeonard.com or www.AllThingsT.com.

Chapter 24:

1. Le Central calls itself "The Affordable French Restaurant" and was established in 1981. If you're familiar at all with how much turnover there is among restaurants in downtown Denver, you realize that 25 plus years in business is remarkable accomplishment for Le Central.

   Located at 112 E 8th Ave Denver, Colorado, reservations are strongly recommended. You can find more information about them – including how they stand for something bold, in a completely unsnooty way - at their website at www.LeCentral.com. Or call them direct at 303-863-8094 to tell them you saw them in this book. Thank you to Jon and Laurie Weiss for introducing us to Le Central.

Chapter 25:

1. Aesop is generally accepted as a man of African descent who lived in Ancient Greece. His fables are usually short stories with a moral lesson, especially for children and often involving talking animals.

   Some of the most popular of Aesop's Fables have found their way into our everyday language, even though many people aren't aware they originated with Aesop. Some of these include "The Tortoise and the Hare," "The Boy Who Cried Wolf," "The Fox and the Grapes" and the fable paraphrased in this chapter called "The Sun and the Wind." There is no definitive website dedicated to Aesop's Fables, however if you visit Google.com and search under "Aesop", you will find lots of different sources.

Chapter 26:

1. The book called "The Peter Principle" by Dr. Laurence Peter is often credited as giving rise to the popular modern cartoon about life in the corporate world, called 'Dilbert.'

2. Visit www.MoneyMeaningandBeyond.com/cleansweep/ to take the Clean-Sweep assessment online.

Chapter 27:

1. To learn more about the Total Immersion style of swimming "as much like a fish as is humanly possible," visit their website at www.TotalImmersion.net or grab a copy of the book "Total Immersion: The Revolutionary Way to Swim Better, Faster and Easier" by TI founder Terry Laughlin

About the Authors

ANDREA J. LEE

Andrea's experience with small businesses started at age 11 when she helped her Dad sort receipts and enter them by hand into a blue ledger book.

Since then she has helped businesses around the world reach six and seven figure financial success while creating lives rich with meaning and laughter.

Along with her previous print publications, "Multiple Streams of Coaching Income" and "Pink Spoon Marketing™" (also with Tina Forsyth), Andrea mentors, teaches, coaches and writes from her home in Calgary, Alberta.

Having run multiple businesses of her own since 1997, Andrea loves her work – and – never likes to be too far from her husband Mike, two Vizslas Chili and Reka or her ping pong club.

Andrea continues to be a thought-leader in the field of personal and business coaching and is writing two new titles for coaches to be released in the next year.

TINA FORSYTH

Tina's first foray into the business world was at age 8, when she used her trusty tape recorder to create a radio commercial for her family's rental business. (Funnily enough they didn't use it.)

Since then, she has been a 'Jill of all Trades' working in everything from marketing to recruiting for businesses big and small. For the past six years she has helped to launch, build and manage over seven 6-figure online businesses.

She is co-author of 'Pink Spoon Marketing'™ (also with Andrea Lee) and a Partner in MultipleStreamsofCoachingIncome.com, MultipleStreamsTeam.com and GrowYourVABiz.com.

Now CEO of OnlineBusinessManager.com, Tina writes and consults in advanced online marketing and business systems for business owners and their support teams.

When you can drag her away from her computer you can find Tina at home in Calgary, Alberta with her husband Dan, daughter Samantha, dog Katy and noisy cat Shadow.

You can reach Tina at tina@onlinebusinessmanager.com or read her blog at www.OnlineBusinessManager.com.

Printed in the United States
50448LVS00003B/97-255